Presented

to

_____

from

D1714996

_____

occasion

_____

date

_____

_____

INCORPORATED
IN YOUR LIFE, JOB AND BUSINESS

The Bible INCORPORATED

IN YOUR LIFE, JOB AND BUSINESS

© Copyright 1988 by Hidden Manna, Inc.
All rights reserved
Printed in the United States of America

Published By:
Hidden Manna, Inc.
P.O. Box 807   Mt. Juliet, TN 37122
(615) 754-0937

Compiled and Written By:
Michael Q. Pink

Cover Design By:
Mark Herron Productions

For seminar information contact publishers at the above address.

Burg. — ISBN 0-9621491-0-1
Mauve — ISBN 0-9621491-2-8
Gray — ISBN 0-9621491-3-6
Lex.—ISBN 1-877994-07-3

DEDICATION

To my Lord, my Counsellor and my closest Friend, Jesus Christ, the Author and Finisher of my faith, and the real Author and Finisher of this book.

And

To my wife, my sweetheart, and next closest friend, Brenda, whose unselfish love and constant encouragement prayed me through the many long hours of research and writing.

With Special Thanks To...

Larry and Jennifer, who helped make this dream possible...Thanks!

TABLE OF CONTENTS:

Keys For Success In Business:

Wisdom In Money Management:

SECTION II:

REAL ANSWERS FOR
REAL LIFE SITUATIONS

Things To Remember When...

What To Do When You Feel...

What You Should Know When...

What To Do When...

What The Bible Says About...

SECTION III:

*EXPERIENCING GOD'S LOVE
IN A TROUBLED WORLD* *237*

Discovering God:

Walking With God:

The Power Of God:

The Love Of God:

INTRODUCTION

This book extracts the counsel of God from Genesis to Revelation on a wide variety of business and work related topics. It then compiles and consolidates the various scriptures into a smooth flowing letter format as if One Person wrote it all. We, of course, recognize the Divine inspiration for the Word of God as coming from one Source, and therefore, the continuity of the Holy Scriptures should be no surprise.

As you read through a given topic, it is fascinating to see the harmony that exists, even though the beginning of a paragraph may have been written some 2,000 years before the last sentence included in that same paragraph. The wisdom of God is given to us by Champions of Faith who acquired this wisdom through practical application of God's known word. They include kings and ranchers, architects and farmers, judges, fishermen, contractors, and even a doctor. The principles they lived by and the truths they held fast are now shared in open view for all to see.

The King James Version was the primary translation used. Where necessary, 20th century words or phrases having the same meaning were substituted to be more readily comprehended by today's reader. For example, the word "ye" was written "you". Also, in I Peter 2:12, we are admonished to have "our conversation honest among the Gentiles." The word conversation is not referring specifically to our speech, but rather our life conduct, or lifestyle, and is quoted instead like this, "having an honest lifestyle among the Gentiles." Great care was given to maintaining the accuracy of the Word of God, and no compromises were made. There were, however, occasional words interjected to connect two or more scriptures such as "and", "for", "remember", etc. Nevertheless, every scripture quoted is marked with a footnote and referenced to enable you to read the entire passage in its original context from the version of your choice.

I trust this book will become an invaluable reference tool of Biblical principles that we may all incorporate into our life, job and business.

Michael Q. Pink
Compiler

SECTION I

TIMELESS PRINCIPLES
AND
PRACTICAL WISDOM

1

CHAPTER 1

THE KEY OF HONESTY

Provide things honest in the sight of all men,[1] and in the sight of the Lord,[2] having an honest lifestyle among the Gentiles, and when they speak against you as evildoers, they may by your good works, which they will see, glorify God in the day of visitation.[3]

If anyone is found guilty of deceiving his neighbor about something entrusted to him, or finding lost property and lying about it, or stealing from his neighbor or cheating him, he shall make full restitution and pay a 20% fine to the one he has wronged.[4] Therefore, do not steal, neither deal falsely, neither lie to each other.[5] Only a false witness will utter lies, for a faithful witness will not lie.[6] So lie not one to another[7] against the truth,[8] and deceive not with your lips,[9] for you have put off the old man with his deeds.[7] Although the bread of deceit is sweet to a man, afterwards his mouth shall be filled with gravel,[10] for the Lord abhors the bloody and deceitful man,[11] and he shall not live out half of his days.[12]

O man, this is good, what the Lord requires

of you, that you do justly, and love mercy and walk humbly with your God.[13]

Though a just man falls seven times, he rises again,[14] for his way is uprightness,[15] and he walks in his integrity[16] and blessings are upon his head.[17] His path is as the shining light that shines more and more unto the perfect day.[18] His tongue is as choice silver,[19] and he will come out of trouble.[20] He will live by faith,[21] and the wealth of the sinner is laid up for him.[22]

Blessed is the man that makes the Lord his trust, and respects not the proud nor such as turn aside to lies.[23] For he knows that the mouth of them that speak lies shall be stopped,[24] and perish,[25] and a false witness shall not be unpunished.[26] Yes he knows that these six things does the Lord hate; yea seven things are an abomination unto Him: A proud look, a lying tongue, hands that shed innocent blood, a heart that plans wicked imaginations, feet that are swift in running to mischief, a false witness that speaks lies, and he that sows discord among the brethren.[27]

Now, if a man vows a vow unto the Lord, or swears an oath to bind his soul with a bond; then he shall not break his word, but he shall do according to all that proceeded out of his mouth.[28] Know this, that the cowardly, the unbelieving, the vile, the murderers, the whoremongers, the sorcerers, the idolaters and all liars shall have their part in the lake which burns with fire and brimstone; which is the second death.[29] And he that says he knows the Lord, but doesn't keep His commandments, is a liar, and the truth is not in him.[30]

Finally brethren, let us walk honestly[31] toward them that are without, that you may have lack of nothing.[32]

References:

*1) Romans 12:17 2) II Corinthians 8:21 3) I Peter 2:12
4) Leviticus 5:16 5) Leviticus 19:11 6) Proverbs 14:5
7) Colossians 3:9 8) James 3:14 9) Proverbs 24:28
10) Proverbs 20:17 11) Psalms 5:6 12) Psalms 55:23
13) Micah 6:8 14) Proverbs 24:16 15) Isaiah 26:7
16) Proverbs 20:7 17) Proverbs 10:6 18) Proverbs 4:18
19) Proverbs 10:20 20) Proverbs 12:13 21) Habakkuk 2:4
22) Proverbs 13:22 23) Psalms 40:4 24) Psalms 63:11
25) Proverbs 19:9 26) Proverbs 19:5 27) Proverbs 6:16-19
28) Numbers 30:2 29) Revelation 21:8 30) I John 2:4
31) Romans 13:13 32) I Thessalonians 4:12*

CHAPTER 2

THE KEY OF TRUST

As for God, His way is perfect; the word of the Lord is tried and true; he is a buckler[1] and horn of salvation[2] to all them that trust in him. Yes He is a high tower, a shield, your refuge and savior that saves you from violence when in Him you trust.[1]

Offer sacrifices of righteousness, put your trust in the Lord,[3] rejoice and ever shout for joy, because He defends you,[4] never leaving you forsaken,[5] but blesses you.[6] He saves with His right hand them which put their trust in Him, from those that rise up against them.[7] Oh, how great is the goodness which God has laid up for them that fear Him; which He has wrought for them that trust in Him;[8] they will not be ashamed; neither shall their enemies triumph over them.[9] In fact, no one that trusts in Him shall be desolate.[10]

Trust in the Lord, and do good, so shall you dwell in the land, and be fed. Commit your way unto the Lord; trust also in Him and He shall bring it to pass.[11] Trust in God at all times;[12] do not be afraid of what man can do to you.[13] For it is better to trust in the Lord than to put confidence in man[14] or princes.[15] In fact, the fear of man brings a snare; but whoever trusts in the Lord shall be safe[16] and be made fat.[17]

Trust in the Lord with all your heart, lean not unto your own understanding. In all your ways acknowledge Him and He shall direct your paths.[18] When you trust in lying words, they cannot profit,[19] but trust in the LORD JEHOVAH for He is everlasting strength,[20] your stronghold in the time of trouble, and He knows them that trust in Him.[21]

Trust in God's word, and you will have what you need to answer him who reproaches you,[22] and you will be like Mount Zion, which cannot be removed, but abides forever.[23]

Do not trust in chariots or horses,[24] or in uncertain riches,[25] or even in yourself; but in God which raises the dead.[26] Yes trust in the mercy of God forever and ever,[27] and remember that without faith it is impossible to please Him, for he that comes to God must believe that He is, and that He is a rewarder of them that diligently seek Him.[28]

References:

1) *II Samuel 22:3* 2) *II Samuel 22:31* 3) *Psalms 4:5*
4) *Psalms 5:11* 5) *Psalms 9:10* 6) *Psalms 2:12*
7) *Psalms 17:7* 8) *Psalms 31:19* 9) *Psalms 25:2*
10) *Psalms 34:22* 11) *Psalms 37:3,5*
12) *Psalms 62:8* 13) *Psalms 56:11* 14) *Psalms 118:8*
15) *Psalms 118:9* 16) *Proverbs 29:25* 17) *Proverbs 28:25*
18) *Proverbs 3:5,6* 19) *Jeremiah 7:8* 20) *Isaiah 26:4*
21) *Nahum 1:7* 22) *Psalms 119:42* 23) *Psalms 125:1*
24) *Psalms 20:7* 25) *I Timothy 6:17*
26) *II Corinthians 1:9* 27) *Psalms 52:8*
28) *Hebrews 11:6*

CHAPTER 3

THE KEY OF RESPECT

Do not be partial to the poor or favor the wealthy in judgement, but in righteousness shall you judge.[1] Respect the covenant,[2] meditate in God's precepts, and respect His way[3] and statutes continually.[4] It is not good to have respect of persons in judgement,[5] for there is no respect of persons with God.[6] If you show special respect to him that wears fine clothing, and say to him, 'sit here in a good place,' and then say to the poor, 'stand over there,' or 'sit here under my footstool,' are you then not partial in yourselves, and become judges of evil thoughts? Listen, has not God chosen the poor of this world, rich in faith, and heirs of the kindgom which he has promised to them that love Him?[7]

Let nothing be done through strife or conceit; but in lowliness of mind let each esteem the other better than themselves.[8] Be kindly affectioned one to another with brotherly love; in honor preferring one another,[9] rendering therefore to all their dues: tribute to whom tribute is due; custom to whom custom; respect to whom respect and honor to whom honor.[10] Let the elders that rule well

be counted worthy of double honor, especially they who labor in the word and doctrine.[11] Honor all men. Love the brotherhood.
Fear God. Honor the king.[12]

Those who do not regard the works of the Lord
nor the operation of His hands, He will destroy and not build them up.[13] He that
regards reproof shall be honored[14] and is prudent,[15] therefore esteem all His precepts.[16]

Honor and respect your father and mother
that your days may be long upon the land
which the Lord your God gives you.[17] Rise
in the presence of the aged, show respect for
the face of an old man and fear your God.[18]
And those that honor God, He will honor,
but they that despise God shall be lightly
esteemed.[19] So honor the Lord with your
substance and with the firstfruits of all
your increase.[20]

All men should honor the Son, even as they
honor the Father. He that honors not the
Son honors not the Father which sent
Him.[21] Also, reverence God's sanctuary; He
is the Lord.[22] Furthermore we have had
fathers of our flesh which corrected (us) and
we gave (them) reverence: shall we not
much rather be in subjection unto the
Father of spirits, and live? Wherefore we
receiving a kingdom which cannot be

moved, let us have grace, whereby we may serve God acceptably with reverence and godly fear.[23]

Remember, if you honor yourself, your honor is nothing.[24] Seek the honor that only comes from God.[25]

References:

1) Leviticus 19:15 2) Psalms 74:20 3) Psalms 119:15
4) Psalms 119:117 5) Proverbs 24:23 6) Romans 2:11
7) James 2:3-5 8) Philippians 2:3 9) Romans 12:10
10) Romans 13:7 11) I Timothy 5:17 12) I Peter 2:17
13) Psalms 28:5 14) Proverbs 13:18 15) Proverbs 15:5
16) Psalms 119:128 17) Exodus 20:12 18) Leviticus 19:32
19) I Samuel 2:30 20) Proverbs 3:9 21) John 5:23
22) Leviticus 19:30 23) Hebrews 12:9,28 24) John 8:54
25) John 5:44

CHAPTER 4

THE KEY OF OBEDIENCE

If you are willing and obedient, you shall eat the good of the land.[1] You shall walk after the LORD your God, and fear Him, and keep His commandments, and obey His voice, and you shall serve Him, and cleave unto Him.[2] For if you shall diligently keep all these commandments which I command you, to do them, to love the LORD your God, to walk in all His ways, and to cleave unto Him, then will the LORD drive out all these nations from before you, and you shall possess greater nations and mightier than yourselves. And every place whereon the soles of your feet shall tread shall be yours; from the wilderness and Lebanon, from the river Euphrates, even unto the uttermost sea shall your coast be. There shall no man be able to stand before you; (for) the LORD your God shall lay the fear of you and the dread of you upon all the land that you shall tread upon, as He has said unto you. Behold I set before you this day a blessing and a curse; a blessing if you obey the commandments of the LORD your God, which I command you this day; and a curse, if you will not obey the commandments of the

LORD your God, but turn aside out of the way which I command you this day, to go after other gods, which you have not known.[3]

Though Jesus were a Son, yet learned He obedience by the things which He suffered and being made perfect, He became the author of eternal salvation unto all them that obey Him.[4]

Realize that to whom you yield yourselves servants to obey, his servants you are to whom you obey; whether of sin unto death, or of obedience unto righteousness.[5] So cast down imaginations and every high thing that exalts itself against the knowledge of God, and bring into captivity every thought to the obedience of Christ;[6] and walk in the spirit and you will not fulfill the lust of the flesh.[7]

Study to show yourself approved unto God, a workman that doesn't need to be ashamed, rightly dividing the word of truth;[8] and study to be quiet, and to do your own business, working with your own hands.[9] Servants be obedient to them that are (your) masters according to the flesh, with fear and trembling, in singleness of heart, as unto Christ.[10]

Now therefore, if you obey God's voice and keep His covenant, then you shall be a peculiar treasure unto God above all people.[11] If you obey and serve Him, you will spend your days in prosperity, and your years in pleasures. But if you obey not, you shall perish by the sword and die without knowledge.[12]

Obey them that have the rule over you, and submit yourselves: for they watch for your souls, as they that must give account, that they may do it with joy, and not with grief: for that (is) unprofitable for you.[13] But refuse profane and old wives' fables, and exercise yourself (rather) unto godliness. For bodily exercise profits little: but godliness is profitable unto all things, having promise of the life that now is, and of that which is to come;[14] And herein, exercise yourself to have always a conscience void of offense toward God, and toward (men).[15]

You ought to obey God rather than men[16] and remember that a double minded man is unstable in all his ways[17] and obedience is better than sacrifice.[18]

References:

1) Isaiah 1:19 2) Deuteronomy 13:4
3) Deuteronomy 11:22-28 4) Hebrews 5:8,9
5) Romans 6:16 6) II Corinthians 10:5
7) Galatians 5:16 8) II Timothy 2:15
9) I Thessalonians 4:11 10) Ephesians 6:5
11) Exodus 19:5 12) Job 36:11,12 13) Hebrews 13:17
14) I Timothy 4:7,8 15) Acts 24:16 16) Acts 5:29
17) James 1:8 18) I Samuel 15:22

CHAPTER 5

THE KEY OF HUMILITY

Humble yourselves in the sight of the Lord, and He shall lift you up.[1] By humility and the fear of the Lord are riches, and honor and life.[2] In fact, humility comes before honor.[3] So be subject one to another, and be clothed with humility: for God resists the proud and gives grace to the humble.[4]

Put on therefore, as the elect of God, holy and beloved, bowels of mercies, kindness, humbleness of mind, meekness, longsuffering, forbearing one another and forgiving one another.[5] For the meek will He guide in judgement: and the meek will He teach His way.[6] For the Lord lifts up the meek.[7] He will beautify them with salvation,[8] they shall inherit the earth,[9] eat and be satisfied,[10] and increase their joy in the Lord.[11]

When pride comes, it brings contention[12] and then shame.[13] Pride goes before destruction, and a haughty spirit before a fall,[14] but the haughty shall be humbled,[15] and brought down.[16] The fear of the Lord is to hate evil: pride, arrogancy, the evil way and perverted speech God hates.[17] In fact, the Lord will cut off all flattering lips, and the tongue that speaks proud things.[18] Yes, He will plentifully reward the proud doer.[19]

Receive with meekness the engrafted word, which is able to save your soul,[20] and show all meekness unto all men.[21] Who among you is wise and endued with knowledge? Let him show it by his good life with meekness of wisdom.[22] Walk worthy of the vocation wherewith you are called, with all lowliness and meekness, with longsuffering, forbearing one another in love.[23]

The Lord will destroy the house of the proud,[24] for everyone that is proud in heart is an abomination to the Lord.[25] So rather let nothing be done through strife or conceit; but in lowliness of mind let each esteem the other as better than themselves.[26] Though the Lord be high, yet has He respect unto the lowly.[27] With the lowly is wisdom,[28] and those that be low will be set up on high;[29] for God gives grace to the lowly,[30] exalting him and abasing him that is high.[31]

References:

1) James 4:10 2) Proverbs 22:4 3) Proverbs 15:33
4) I Peter 5:5 5) Colossians 3:12,13 6) Psalms 25:9
7) Psalms 147:6 8) Psalms 149:4 9) Psalms 37:11
10) Psalms 22:26 11) Isaiah 29:19 12) Proverbs 13:10
13) Proverbs 11:2 14) Proverbs 16:18 15) Isaiah 10:33
16) II Samuel 22:28 17) Proverbs 8:13 18) Psalms 12:3
19) Psalms 31:23 20) James 1:21 21) Titus 3:2
22) James 3:13 23) Ephesians 4:1 24) Proverbs 15:25
25) Proverbs 16:5 26) Philippians 2:3 27) Psalms 138:6
28) Proverbs 11:2 29) Job 5:11 30) Proverbs 3:34
31) Ezekiel 21:26

CHAPTER 6

THE KEY
OF COMMITMENT

Take heed to the ministry which you receive from the Lord, that you fulfill it.[1] For unto whomsoever much is given, of him shall much be required: and to them who have been entrusted with much, much more will be asked.[2]

God is able to keep that which you commit to him.[3] If you commit your way unto the Lord, and trust also in Him; He will bring it to pass.[4] Commit your works unto the Lord and He will establish your thoughts;[5] yes, unto God commit your cause.[6] Commit the keeping of your soul to God, and do good, as unto a faithful Creator.[7]

If a man vow a vow unto the Lord, or swear an oath to bind his soul with a bond; he shall not break his word, he shall do according to all that proceeds out of his mouth.[8] When you vow a vow unto the Lord your God, you shall not slack to pay it: for the Lord your God will surely require it of you; and it would be sin in you.[9] But if you choose not to vow, it won't be sin to you.[10] When you vow a vow unto God, defer not to pay it; for He has no pleasure in fools: pay that which you have vowed. Better is it that you shouldn't vow than to make a vow and not fulfill it.[11] So will I sing praise unto His name forever, that I may daily perform my vows.[12] God honors those who will keep their commitment even when it hurts.[13]

All Judah rejoiced at the oath: for they had sworn with all their heart, and sought Him with their whole desire; and He was found of them: and the Lord gave them rest round about.[14]

Model of Commitment:

Looking unto Jesus the author and finisher of our faith; who for the joy that was set before Him endured the cross, despising the shame, and is set down at the right hand of the throne of God.[15]

References:

1) Colossians 4:17 2) Luke 12:48 3) II Timothy 1:12
4) Psalms 37:5 5) Proverbs 16:3 6) Job 5:8
7) I Peter 4:19 8) Numbers 30:2 9) Deuteronomy 23:21
10) Deuteronomy 23:22 11) Ecclesiastes 5:4,5
12) Psalms 66:13 13) Psalms 15:4 14) II Chronicles 15:15
15) Hebrews 12:2

CHAPTER 7

THE KEY OF INTEGRITY

The just man walks in his integrity and it guides him and his children are blessed;[1] but the perverseness of transgressors shall destroy them.[2] Wait on God, and let integrity and uprightness preserve you.[3]

Because of the integrity of Abimelech's heart, God protected him from sinning against God with Abraham's wife.[4] David also walked in integrity and God redeemed him and was merciful to him,[5] upholding him and promised to keep him before His face forever[6] not letting him slide.[7]

Job held fast his integrity, and when Satan moved against him without cause,[8] Job still said "Till I die I will not remove mine integrity from me.[9] Let me be weighed in an even balance that God may know mine integrity."[10]

It is better to be poor and walk in integrity than to be perverse in your lips and be a fool.[11]

References:

1) Proverbs 20:7 2) Proverbs 11:3 3) Psalms 25:21
4) Genesis 20:6 5) Psalms 26:11 6) Psalms 41:12
7) Psalms 26:1 8) Job 2:3 9) Job 27:5 10) Job 31:6
11) Proverbs 19:1

CHAPTER 8

THE KEY OF ENDURANCE

Thou therefore endure hardness and afflictions[1] as a good soldier of Jesus Christ[2] knowing that after you have patiently endured[3] in faith you will inherit the promise.[4] Call to remembrance the former days in which after you were illuminated, you endured a great fight of afflictions[5] and cast not away therefore your confidence which has great recompense of reward.[6]

Look unto Jesus, the author and finisher of your faith; who for the joy that was set before Him, endured the cross, despising the shame, and is set down at the right hand of the throne of God.[7] The Lord[8] and His word[9] shall endure forever. In fact, His name,[10] His glory,[11] His truth,[12] righteousness,[13] praise,[14] mercy[15] and goodness endure forever to all generations, continually.[16]

So continue in prayer,[17] and in the faith and love and holiness with sobriety,[18] knowing that through much tribulation we enter into the Kingdom of God.[19] Continue in the love of Jesus[20] and the grace of God,[21] and if you also continue in His word, then are you His

20

disciples indeed.[22]

Don't be like the ones with no root in themselves, who endure for a time, but afterward, when affliction or persecution arises for the word's sake, immediately they are offended;[23] for you shall be hated of all men for my name's sake: but he that shall endure unto the end, the same shall be saved.[24]

Persecutions and afflictions will come, but endure them, for the Lord will deliver you out of them all.[25] With God's love you can bear all things, believe all things, hope all things and endure all things[26] knowing that after you have endured temptation, and when you are tried, you shall receive the crown of life, which the Lord has promised to them that love Him[27] and happy shall you be.[28]

References:

1) II Timothy 4:5 2) II Timothy 2:3 3) Hebrews 6:15
4) Hebrews 6:12 5) Hebrews 10:32 6) Hebrews 10:35
7) Hebrews 12:2 8) Psalms 9:7 9) I Peter 1:25
10) Psalms 72:17 11) Psalms 104:31 12) Psalms 100:5
13) Psalms 111:3 14) Psalms 111:10 15) I Chronicles 16:34
16) Psalms 52:1 17) Colossians 4:2 18) I Timothy 2:15
19) Acts 14:22 20) John 15:9 21) Acts 13:43
22) John 8:31 23) Mark 4:17 24) Mark 13:13
25) II Timothy 3:11 26) I Corinthians 13:7
27) James 1:12 28) James 5:11

CHAPTER 9

THE KEY OF STRENGTH

When the Lord is your strength, who is there to be afraid of?[1] He is the saving strength of His anointed.[2] Seek the Lord and His strength and seek His face continually[3] and He will be your strength and power, making your way perfect.[4] The Lord is our rock, our fortress, our deliverer, our God and our strength in whom we will trust.[5] He girds us with strength,[6] and the joy of the Lord becomes our strength.[7]

The Lord will give strength unto His people,[8] yes strength and power,[9] enabling them to go from strength to strength.[10] But a horse is a vain thing for safety: neither shall he deliver any by his great strength,[11] for God doesn't delight in the strength of a horse nor does He take pleasure in the legs of man.[12] Be strong in the Lord and in the power of His might[13] and in the grace that is in Christ Jesus.[14] Then you will be strengthened with all might, according to His glorious power[15] and able to do all things through Christ who strengthens you,[16] because greater is He that is in you than he that is in the world.[17] For we are the circumcision, which worship

God in the Spirit, and rejoice in Christ Jesus, having no confidence in the flesh.[18] For God's grace is sufficient for you, for His strength is made perfect in weakness. Most gladly therefore boast about your weaknesses, that the power of Christ may rest upon you.[19]

Be strong and very courageous, fear not, for the Lord thy God is with you; He will not fail you nor forsake you.[20] If you faint in the day of adversity, your strength is small,[21] so don't be weary in well doing, for in due season, you shall reap, if you faint not.[22] And besides, God gives power to the faint, and to them that have no might, He increases strength. But they that wait upon the Lord shall renew their strength; they shall mount up with wings as eagles; they shall run and not be weary; and they shall walk and not faint.[23] He will make their feet like hinds' feet, and He will make them to walk upon high places.[24]

The eyes of the Lord run to and fro throughout the whole earth, to show Himself strong in the behalf of them whose heart is perfect toward Him.[25] Let the weak say, I am strong,[26] for whoever executes God's word is strong.[27] Fear not, God is with you. Be not dismayed for He is your God. He will strengthen you, yes He will help you, yes He will uphold you with the right hand of His righteousness.[28] Just wait on the Lord, and be of good courage, and He will strengthen your heart,[29] all you that hope in the Lord.[30] For God increases His people greatly, making them stronger than their enemies,[31] and he that has clean hands, will be stronger and stronger.[32]

When you are weak in the flesh, then you are strong in the Lord,[33] and He will be your strength in the time of trouble.[34] Remember that glory and honor are in His presence; strength and gladness are in His place.[35]

References:

*1) Psalms 27:1 2) Psalms 28:8 3) I Chronicles 16:11
4) II Samuel 22:33 5) Psalms 18:2 6) Psalms 18:32
7) Nehemiah 8:10 8) Psalms 29:11 9) Psalms 68:35
10) Psalms 84:7 11) Psalms 33:17 12) Psalms 147:10
13) Ephesians 6:10 14) II Timothy 2:1
15) Colossians 1:11 16) Philippians 4:13
17) I John 4:4 18) Philippians 3:3
19) II Corinthians 12:9 20) Deuteronomy 31:6
21) Proverbs 24:10 22) Galatians 6:9
23) Isaiah 40:29, 31 24 Habakkuk 3:19
25) II Chronicles 16:9 26) Joel 3:10 27) Joel 2:11
28) Isaiah 41:10 29) Psalms 27:14 30) Psalms 31:24
31) Psalms 105:24 32) Job 17:9 33) II Corinthians 12:10
34) Psalms 37:39 35) I Chronicles 16:27*

CHAPTER 10

THE KEY OF AMBITION/
PURPOSE IN LIFE

Seek ye first the kingdom of God, and His
righteousness, and all these things shall be
added unto you.[1] In all your ways acknowledge Him, and he will direct your
paths,[2] and commit your works unto the
Lord and your thoughts will be established.[3]
For what does the Lord require of you, but to
do justly, and to love mercy, and to walk
humbly with your God.[4]

Write the vision, and make it plain upon
tablets, that he may run that reads it. For the
vision is for an appointed time, but at the
end it shall speak and not lie: though it tarry,
wait for it; because it will surely come, it will
not tarry.[5] For where there is no vision the
people perish.[6]

God will fulfill the desire of them that fear
Him,[7] yes the desire of the righteous shall be
granted,[8] for the desire of the righteous is
only good[9] and the desire accomplished is
sweet to the soul.[10] But brethren, rather give
diligence to make your calling and election

sure,[11] knowing that the gifts and calling of God are without repentance.[12] Only let every man abide in the same calling wherein he was called.[13]

Pray to have the eyes of your understanding enlightened, that you may know what is the hope of His calling,[14] to which you are called.[15] For He has saved you and called you with a holy calling, not according to your works, but according to His own purpose and grace.[16] You are called according to His purpose,[17] who works all things after the counsel of His own will,[18] as partakers of the heavenly calling[19] to fear the Lord your God, to walk in all His ways, and to love Him, and to serve the Lord your God with all your heart, and with all your soul.[20]

A dream comes through the multitude of business,[21] but follow after love, and desire spiritual gifts,[22] delighting yourself in the Lord and He will give you the desires of your heart.[23] Every purpose is established by counsel,[24] and there is a time for every purpose under the heavens[25] and for every good work.[26]

Brethren, do this one thing, forget those things which are behind, reach forth unto those things which are ahead, and press toward the mark for the prize of the high calling of God in Christ Jesus,[27] and remember anyone wanting to be the greatest must be the least - the servant of all.[28]

References:

*1) Matthew 6:33 2) Proverbs 3:6 3) Proverbs 16:3
4) Micah 6:8 5) Habakkuk 2:2–3 6) Proverbs 29:18
7) Psalms 145:19 8) Proverbs 10:24 9) Proverbs 11:23
10) Proverbs 13:19 11) II Peter 1:10 12) Romans 11:29
13) I Corinthians 7:20 14) Ephesians 1:18
15) Ephesians 4:4 16 II Timothy 1:9 17) Romans 8:28
18) Ephesians 1:11 19) Hebrews 3:1
20) Deuteronomy 10:12 21) Ecclesiastes 5:3
22) I Corinthians 14:1 23) Psalms 37:4
24) Proverbs 20:18 25) Ecclesiastes 3:1
26) Ecclesiastes 3:17 27) Philippians 3:13–14
28) Mark 9:35*

CHAPTER 11

THE KEY OF LOYALTY

If you are faithful over a few things, God will make you ruler over many[1] because he that is faithful in that which is least is faithful also in much: and he that is unjust in the least is unjust also in much.[2]

A faithful witness is hard to find.[3] He will not lie[4] or reveal secrets[5] and is like the cold of snow at harvest time; he refreshes the soul of his masters[6] and is health to them.[7] The Lord preserves the faithful,[8] and he shall abound with blessings,[9] but the proud doer shall be harshly punished.[8]

It is required in stewards that a man be found faithful,[10] and whatever he does to brothers or strangers, it should be done faithfully.[11] If a wise and faithful servant is put in charge of his lord's household, and faithfully executes that responsibility until his lord returns, he shall be made ruler over all his goods.[12]

References:

1) Matthew 25:21   2) Luke 16:10   3) Proverbs 20:6
4) Proverbs 14:5   5) Proverbs 11:3   6) Proverbs 25:13
7) Proverbs 13:17   8) Psalms 31:23   9) Proverbs 28:20
10) I Corinthians 4:2   11) III John 1:5   12) Matthew 24:45,46

CHAPTER 12

THE KEY OF PERSEVERANCE

Praying always with all prayer and supplication in the Spirit, and watching there-
unto with all perseverance and supplication
for all saints.[1] Men ought always to pray,
and not to faint,[2] though our outward man
perish, the inward man is renewed day by
day.[3]

Brethren, be not weary in well doing,[4] for
God has satiated the weary soul, and has
replenished every sorrowful soul.[5] Only be
thou strong and very courageous, that you
may observe to do according to all the law,
which Moses, God's servant commanded
you: turn not from it to the right hand or the
left, that you may prosper wherever you go.[6]
Do not turn aside from following the Lord,
but serve the Lord with all your heart.[7]

Continue in the words of Jesus, then are you
His disciple indeed,[8] and as the Father has
loved Jesus, so Christ has loved you, so continue in His love,[9] and in the grace of God.[10]
Turn to your God: keep mercy and judgement, and wait on your God continually,[11]

and He shall renew your strength; you shall mount up with wings as eagles; you shall run, and not be weary; you shall walk and not faint.[12]

Continue in the things which you have learned and have been assured of,[13] and unto the doctrine, and you shall save yourself and them that hear you.[14] Even women shall be saved in childbearing, if they continue in faith and charity and holiness with sobriety.[15] Jesus will present you holy and unblamable and unreprovable in His sight if you continue in the faith grounded and settled, and be not moved away from the hope of the gospel, which you have heard.[16]

Continue in the faith, for it is through much tribulation that we must enter into the kingdom of God.[17] So continue in prayer, watch in thanksgiving,[18] and don't be weary in well doing: for in due season you shall reap, if you faint not.[19]

References:

1) *Ephesians 6:18* 2) *Luke 18:1* 3) *II Corinthians 4:16*
4) *II Thessalonians 3:13* 5) *Jeremiah 31:25* 6) *Joshua 1:7*
7) *I Samuel 12:20* 8) *John 8:31* 9) *John 15:9*
10) *Acts 13:43* 11) *Hosea 12:6* 12) *Isaiah 40:31*
13) *II Timothy 3:14* 14) *I Timothy 4:16*
15) *I Timothy 2:15* 16) *Colossians 1:22,23*
17) *Acts 14:22* 18) *Colossians 4:2* 19) *Galatians 6:9*

CHAPTER 13

THE KEY OF
A WINNING ATTITUDE

You can do all things through Christ who strengthens you[1] because greater is He that is in you than he that is in the world.[2] In fact, whatsoever is born of God, overcometh the world, and this is the victory that overcometh the world, even our faith.[3] He that overcomes the world is he that believes that Jesus is the Son of God.[4]

Be not overcome of evil, but overcome evil with good.[5] To him that overcomes, God will give to eat of the tree of life, which is in the midst of the paradise of God.[6] He will not be hurt by the second death,[7] but rather eat of the hidden manna, and receive a white stone with a new name written, which no man knows except he that receives it.[8] He will also be clothed with white raiment, and instead of his name being blotted out of the book of life, Jesus will confess his name before the Father and before His angels.[9]

Give thanks unto God, which always causes us to triumph in Christ[10] knowing that no weapon formed against you will prosper, and every tongue that rises up against you in judgement you shall condemn for this is the heritage of the servants of the Lord.[11]

With God's help you can run through a troop, leap over a wall,[12] and triumph in the works of your hands,[13] so run that you may obtain.[14] Thanks be to God which gives you the victory[15] and makes you more than a conqueror, through our Lord Jesus Christ.[16]

Many are the afflictions of the righteous, but the Lord delivers him out of them all.[17] So, clap your hands and shout unto God with a voice of triumph[18] who brings us great victory.[19] O sing unto the Lord a new song, for He hath done marvelous things; His right hand, and His holy arm, hath gotten him the victory.[20]

He that winneth souls is wise,[21] and you that overcome will be a pillar in the temple of God,[22] be seated with Christ in His throne,[23] inherit all things and be God's son and He will be your God.[24]

Remember, count all things but loss for the excellency of the knowledge of Christ Jesus, counting everything you lose as dung, that you may win Christ.[25]

References:

1) Philippians 4:13   2) I John 4:4   3) I John 5:4
4) I John 5:5   5) Romans 12:21   6) Revelation 2:7
7) Revelation 2:11   8) Revelation 2:17   9) Revelation 3:5
10) II Corinthians 2:14   11) Isaiah 54:17
12) Psalms 18:29   13) Psalms 92:4   14) I Corinthians 9:24
15) I Corinthians 15:57   16) Romans 8:37
17) Psalms 34:19   18) Psalms 47:1   19) II Samuel 23:12
20) Psalms 98:1   21) Proverbs 11:30   22) Revelation 3:12
23) Revelation 3:21   24) Revelation 21:7
25) Philippians 3:8

CHAPTER 14

THE KEY OF
A BALANCED
TEMPERAMENT

Cease from anger, forsake wrath, and quit worrying - it only leads to evil.[1] Let all bitterness and wrath and anger and clamor and evil speaking be put away from you with all malice[2] and blasphemy and put filthy communication out of your mouth.[3]

Be not hasty in spirit to be angry,[4] for he that angers quickly deals foolishly.[5] Good sense makes a man slow to anger,[6] and he that is slow to anger is better than the mighty,[7] he appeases strife[8] and is of great understanding.[9] Wrath is cruel, and anger is outrageous,[10] but a soft answer will turn wrath away.[11] Make no friendship with an angry man; and with a furious man, you should not go,[12] for an angry man stirs up strife, and a furious man abounds in transgression,[13] and a man of great wrath shall suffer punishment,[14] but wise men know how to turn away wrath.[15]

Dearly beloved, avenge not yourselves, but rather give place unto wrath: for it is written, Vengeance is mine; I will repay, saith the Lord.[16] But whoever is angry with his brother without cause shall be in danger of the judgement, and whoever shall insult his brother shall be in danger of the council; but whoever shall say 'You fool!' shall be in danger of hell fire.[17]

Keep your tongue from evil, and your lips from speaking guile.[18] In your anger, do not sin; do not let the sun go down upon your wrath.[19] Take heed to your ways that you sin not with your tongue, and keep your mouth with a bridle, while the wicked is before you.[20] Don't you know that death and life are in the power of the tongue, and they that love it shall eat the fruit thereof?[21]

If any man among you seem to be religious, and bridles not his tongue, he deceives his own heart, and his religion is in vain.[22] For whoso keeps his mouth and his tongue, keeps his soul from troubles.[23] If you want long life and good days, refrain your tongue from evil, and your lips that they speak no guile.[24] Add to your knowledge temperance,[25] against such there is no law.[26]

Every man everywhere should lift up holy

hands, without wrath and doubting,[27] and be kind one to another, tenderhearted, forgiving one another, even as God for Christ's sake has forgiven you.[28] Wherefore, my beloved brethren, let every man be swift to hear, slow to speak, slow to wrath; for the wrath of man does not work the righteousness of God.[29]

References:

1) Psalms 37:8   2) Ephesians 4:31   3) Colossians 3:8
4) Ecclesiastes 7:9   5) Proverbs 14:17   6) Proverbs 19:11
7) Proverbs 16:32   8) Proverbs 15:18   9) Proverbs 14:29
10) Proverbs 27:4   11) Proverbs 15:1   12) Proverbs 22:24
13) Proverbs 29:22   14) Proverbs 19:19   15) Proverbs 29:8
16) Romans 12:19   17) Matthew 5:22   18) Psalms 34:13
19) Ephesians 4:26   20) Psalms 39:1   21) Proverbs 18:21
22) James 1:26   23) Proverbs 21:23   24) I Peter 3:10
25) II Peter 1:6   26) Galatians 5:23   27) I Timothy 2:8
28) Ephesians 4:32   29) James 1:19,20

CHAPTER 15

THE KEY OF
GOOD WORK HABITS

Awake early[1] and seek God,[2] for God loves
those that love Him and those that seek Him
early will find Him.[3] A dream comes
through the multitude of business,[4] but
know the state of your flocks, and look well
to thy herds.[5] Labor until the evening,[6] but
don't stay up late, for God gives His beloved
sleep.[7] You will eat the labor of your hands,
and happy shalt thou be, and it shall be well
with thee.[8]

The hand of the diligent maketh rich[9] and
fat,[10] and shall bear rule,[11] tending only to
plenteousness.[12] He shall stand before kings;
he shall not stand before mean men.[13] On
the other hand, the slothful and slack handed sluggard is a brother to him that is a great
waster[14] and will become poor,[9] having
nothing[10] and always under tribute.[11] He
sleeps late opening the door to poverty,[15]
and makes excuses not to work;[16] even his
hands refuse to labor.[17]

Wealth gotten by vanity shall be diminished;

but he that gathereth by labor shall increase,[18] and the labor of the righteous tendeth to life.[19] In all labor there is profit,[20] but don't labor to be rich[21] or for meat which perishes, but labor for that meat which endures unto everlasting life, which the Son of man shall give unto you.[22]

Be not slothful in business, but fervent in spirit, serving the Lord,[23] and whatsoever your hands find to do, do it with thy might[24] not wasting time talking which tends only to penury.[20]

Obey in all things your masters according to the flesh; not with eye service, as men pleasers; but in singleness of heart, fearing God.[25] Let him that stole, steal no more; but rather let him labor, working with his hands the thing which is good, that he may have to give to him that needeth,[26] and receive his own reward according to his labor.[27]

Remember, if any will not work, neither should he eat,[28] and if he doesn't provide for his own, and especially for those of his own house, he hath denied the faith, and is worse than an infidel.[29]

Behold, it is good and comely for one to eat and drink and to enjoy all the good of his labor that he taketh under the sun all the days of his life, which God gives him,[30] for it is the gift of God.[31]

References:

1) Psalms 57:8 2) Psalms 63:1 3) Proverb 8:17
4) Ecclesiastes 5:3 5) Proverbs 27:23
6) Psalms 104:23 7) Psalms 127:2
8) Psalms 128:2 9) Proverbs 10:4
10) Proverbs 13:4 11) Proverbs 12:24
12) Proverbs 21:5 13) Proverbs 22:29
14) Proverbs 18:9 15) Proverbs 6:9
16) Proverbs 22:13 17) Proverbs 21:25
18) Proverbs 13:11 19) Proverbs 10:16
20) Proverb 14:23 21) Proverbs 23:4
22) John 6:27 23) Romans 12:11
24) Ecclesiastes 9:10 25) Colossians 3:22
26) Ephesians 4:28 27) I Corinthians 3:8
28) II Thessalonians 3:10 29) I Timothy 5:8
30) Ecclesiastes 5:18 31) Ecclesiastes 3:13

CHAPTER 16

THE KEY OF
EXCELLENCE

His divine power has given us everything we
need for life and godliness through the
knowledge of Him who called us to glory
and excellence, through which He has given
us very great and precious promises, that by
these you may escape the corruption that is
in the world through lust. For this very
reason, make every effort to add to your
faith excellence; and to excellence, knowledge; and to knowledge, self control; and to
self control, patience and godliness; and to
godliness, brotherly kindness; and to
brotherly kindness, love. For if you possess
these traits in increasing measure, they will
keep you from being ineffective or unfruitful in the knowledge of our Lord Jesus
Christ. Wherefore brethren, make your calling and election sure: for if you do these
things, you will never fall.[1]

If any man speak, let him speak as the
oracles of God; if any minister, let him do it
as of the ability which God gives; that God
in all things may be glorified through Jesus

Christ.[2] And whatever you do in word or deed, do all in the name of the Lord Jesus, giving thanks to God and the Father by Him.[3]

He that has knowledge spares his words; and a man of understanding is of an excellent spirit.[4] The righteous is more excellent than his neighbor,[5] and excellent speech is not appropriate for a fool.[6] Listen to wisdom, for it speaks of excellent things.[7]

Seek that you may excel to the edifying of the church,[8] and whatsoever you do, do it heartily, as to the Lord, and not unto men.[9] Has not the Lord written to you excellent things in counsels and knowledge to make you know the certainty of the words of truth?[10]

Examples of Excellence in Biblical History:

1. And Chenaniah, chief of the Levites, (was) for song: he instructed about the song, because he (was) skillful.[11]

2. Forasmuch as an excellent spirit, and knowledge, and understanding, interpreting of dreams, and showing of hard sentences, and dissolving of doubts, were found in the same Daniel, whom the king named Belte-

shazzar: now let Daniel be called, and he will show the interpretation.[12]

3. Then this Daniel was preferred above the presidents and princes, because an excellent spirit (was) in him; and the king thought to set him over the whole realm.[13]

4. Now therefore command thou that they hew me cedar trees out of Lebanon; and my servants shall be with thy servants: and unto thee will I give hire for thy servants according to all that thou shalt appoint: for thou knowest that (there is) not among us any that can skill to hew timber like unto the Sidonians.[14]

5. As for these children, God gave them knowledge and skill in all learning and wisdom: and Daniel had understanding in all visions and dreams.[15]

6. Children in whom (was) no blemish, but well favored, and skillful in all wisdom, and cunning in knowledge, and understanding science, and such as (had) ability in them to stand in the king's palace, and whom they might teach the learning and the tongue of the Chaldeans.[16]

7. Many daughters have done virtuously, but thou excellest them all.[17]

Approve things which are excellent; that you may be sincere and without offense till the day of Christ,[18] knowing that we have this treasure in earthen vessels, that the excellency of the power may be of God.[19] And remember, by faith, Abel offered unto God a more excellent sacrifice than Cain, by which he obtained witness that he was righteous.[20]

References:

1) II Peter 1:3–8, 10 2) I Peter 4:11 3) Colossians 3:17
4) Proverbs 17:27 5) Proverbs 12:26 6) Proverbs 17:7
7) Proverbs 8:6 8) I Corinthians 14:12 9) Colossians 3:23
10) Proverbs 22:20–21 11) I Chronicles 15:22
12) Daniel 5:12 13) Daniel 6:3 14) I Kings 5:6
15) Daniel 1:17 16) Daniel 1:4 17) Proverbs 31:29
18) Phillippians 1:10 19) II Corinthians 4:7
20) Hebrews 11:4

CHAPTER 17

THE KEY OF KNOWLEDGE

People are destroyed for lack of knowledge.[1]
Those that hate knowledge and choose not
the fear of the Lord shall eat the fruit of their
own way and be filled with their own
devices.[2] Yet if you cry after knowledge and
lift up your voice for understanding, if you
seek her as silver, and search for her like
hidden treasure;[3] then you will understand
the fear of the Lord and find the knowledge
of God. For the Lord gives wisdom, and out
of His mouth come knowledge and understanding.[4]

The fear of the Lord is the beginning of wisdom, and the knowledge of the Holy is
understanding.[5] The heart of him that has
understanding seeks knowledge,[6] and the
heart of the prudent gets knowledge,[7] and
when the wise is instructed he receives
knowledge.[8] Also, that the soul be without
knowledge is not good,[9] so wise men lay up
knowledge,[10] and their tongue dispenses it[11]
and with their lips they disperse it.[12] He who
loves instruction loves knowledge,[13] and he
that has knowledge, spares his words.[14] The
eyes of the Lord preserve knowledge,[15] and

through it the just shall be delivered.[16] Apply your heart unto God's knowledge,[17] and receive His instruction instead of silver, and receive knowledge instead of choice gold.[18] A man of knowledge increases strength,[19] and by knowledge shall the chambers be filled with all precious and pleasant riches.[20]

The Lord is a God of knowledge,[21] and gives to man that is good in His sight wisdom and knowledge and joy.[22] However, if you have all knowledge and have not love, you are nothing,[23] because knowledge by itself puffs up, but love edifies.[24] But thanks be to God, which always causes us to triumph in Christ, and makes known the savor of His knowledge by us in every place;[25] that you might walk worthy of the Lord unto all pleasing, being fruitful in every good work, and increasing in the knowledge of God.[26]

Know that the knowledge of wisdom is good for your soul, and if you find it, there is hope for your future.[27] But in much wisdom is much grief; and he that increases knowledge, increases sorrow.[28]

Notable Biblical Examples:

1. And God said to Solomon, Because this was in thine heart, and thou hast not asked

riches, wealth or honor, nor the life of thine enemies, neither yet hast asked long life, but hast asked wisdom and knowledge for thyself, that thou mayest judge my people, over whom I have made thee king: wisdom and knowledge (is) granted unto thee; and I will give thee riches, and wealth, and honor, such as none of the kings have had that (have been) before thee, neither shall there any after thee have the like.[29]

2. And Hezekiah spoke comfortably unto all the Levites that taught the good knowledge of the Lord: and they did eat throughout the feast seven days, offering peace offerings, and making confession to the Lord God of their fathers.[30]

References:

1) Hosea 4:6 2) Proverbs 1:29,31 3) Proverbs 2:3,4
4) Proverbs 2:5,6 5) Proverbs 9:10 6) Proverbs 15:14
7) Proverbs 18:15 8) Proverbs 21:11 9) Proverbs 19:2
10) Proverbs 10:14 11) Proverbs 15:2 12) Proverbs 15:7
13) Proverbs 12:1 14) Proverbs 17:27 15) Proverbs 22:12
16) Proverbs 11:9 17) Proverbs 22:17 18) Proverbs 8:10
19) Proverbs 24:5 20) Proverbs 24:4 21) I Samuel 2:3
22) Ecclesiastes 2:26 23) I Corinthians 13:2
24) I Corinthians 8:1 25) II Corinthians 2:14
26) Colossians 1:10 27) Proverbs 24:14
28) Ecclesiastes 1:18 29) II Chronicles 1:11,12
30) II Chronicles 30:22

CHAPTER 18

THE KEY OF ABILITY

If any minister, let him do it as of the ability which God gives: that God in all things may be glorified through Jesus Christ.[1] As every man has received special abilities, be sure to use them to serve others, as good stewards of God's grace in its many different forms,[2] knowing that every good and perfect gift is from above and comes down from the Father of lights, with whom there is no changing nor shifting shadows.[3]

Understand, that in you (that is, in your flesh) dwells no good thing,[4] so worship God in the Spirit, and rejoice in Christ Jesus, having no confidence in the flesh,[5] because no flesh should glory in God's presence.[6] Are you so foolish, having begun in the spirit, are you now made perfect in the flesh?[7] God's grace is sufficient for you: for His strength is made perfect in weakness. Most gladly therefore, boast of your weaknesses, so that Christ's power may rest upon you.[8]

It was Jesus who said, "Verily, verily, I say unto you, the Son can do nothing of Himself, but what He sees the Father do: for whatever the Father does, these also the Son does likewise.[9] I can of my own self do nothing: as I hear, I judge: and my judgement is just; because I seek not my own will, but the will of the Father which has sent me.[10] I am the vine, you are the branches. He that abides in me, and I in him, the same brings forth much fruit; for without me you can do nothing."[11]

Biblical Examples:

1. And he informed me, and talked with me, and said, O Daniel, I am now come forth to give thee skill and understanding.[12]

2. Then the disciples, every man according to his ability, determined to send relief unto the brethren which dwelt in Judea.[13]

3. And unto one he gave five talents, to another two, and to another one, to every man according to his several ability: and straightway took his journey.[14]

4. And Cheneniah, chief of the Levites, (was) for song: he instructed because he was skillful.[15]

God girds you with strength, and makes your way perfect[16] and blessed if your strength is in Him.[17] So sing unto the Lord a new song; play skillfully with a loud noise;[18] stir up the gift of God which is in you,[19] knowing that you can do all things through Christ which strengthens you.[20] And remember, a man's gift makes room for him, and brings him before great men.[21]

References:

1) I Peter 4:11   2) I Peter 4:10   3) James 1:17
4) Romans 7:18   5) Philippians 3:3   6) I Corinthians 1:29
7) Galatians 3:3   8) II Corinthians 12:9   9) John 5:19
10) John 5:30   11) John 15:5   12) Daniel 9:22
13) Acts 11:29   14) Matthew 25:15   15) I Chronicles 15:22
16) Psalms 18:32   17) Psalms 84:5   18) Psalms 33:3
9) II Timothy 1:6   20) Philippians 4:13
21) Proverbs 18:16

CHAPTER 19

THE KEY OF PEOPLE SKILLS

A soft answer turns away wrath, but grievous words stir up anger.[1] If it be possible, as much as lies in you, live peaceably with all men,[2] not avenging yourselves, but rather giving place unto wrath: for it is written, "Vengeance is mine; I will repay," saith the Lord.[3] For the wrath of man does not work the righteousness of God.[4] Be angry, and sin not: don't let the sun go down upon your wrath.[5] Agree with your adversary quickly, while on the way to court, lest at any time he delivers you to the judge, and the judge delivers you to the officer and you be cast into prison.[6]

Be kindly affectioned to one another with brotherly love; in honor preferring one another,[7] tenderhearted, forgiving one another, even as God for Christ's sake has forgiven you.[8] Lie not one to another, seeing that you have put off the old man with his deeds,[9] but exhort one another daily, while it is called today; lest any of you be hardened through the deceitfulness of sin.[10] And let us consider one another to provoke unto love and to good works,[11] being of the same mind one toward another. Mind not high things, but condescend to men of low estate. Be not wise in your own conceits, recompensing to no man evil for evil. Provide things honest in the sight of all men.[12] Wherefore receive one another as Christ also received us to the glory of God.[13]

Owe no man anything but to love one another, for he that loves another has fulfilled the law.[14] And let us not therefore judge one another anymore: but judge this rather, that no man put a stumbling block or an occasion to fall in his brother's way.[15] As every man has received the gift, even so minister the same one to another, as good stewards of the manifold grace of God.[16]

Be subject one to another, and be clothed with humility: for God resists the proud, and gives grace to the humble.[17] Bless them which persecute you: bless and curse not. Rejoice with them that do rejoice, and weep with them that weep;[18] forbearing one another, and forgiving one another, if any man has a quarrel against any: even as Christ forgave you, so also forgive.[19] And use hospitality one to another without grudging.[20]

Bear one another's burdens, and so fulfill the law of Christ,[21] and if any man be overtaken in a fault, you which are spiritual, restore such a one in the spirit of meekness, considering yourself, lest you also be tempted.[22] And walk in love, as Christ also has loved us, and given Himself for us as an offering and a sacrifice to God for a sweet smelling savor.[23] For if a man thinks himself to be something when he is nothing, he deceives himself.[24]

Submit yourselves one to another in the fear of God,[25] and confess your faults one to another, and pray for one another, that you may be healed.[26] Take heed to yourselves: if your brother trespasses against you, rebuke him, and if he repent, forgive him,[27] until seventy times seven.[28]

Remember, the patient in spirit is better than the proud in spirit,[29] So let nothing be done through strife or conceit; but in lowliness of mind let each esteem the other better than themselves.[30] Warn them that are unruly, comfort the feebleminded, support the weak and be patient toward all men.[31]

References:

*1) Proverbs 15:1 2) Romans 12:18 3) Romans 12:19
4) James 1:20 5) Ephesians 4:26 6) Matthew 5:25
7) Romans 12:10 8) Ephesians 4:32 9) Colossians 3:9
10) Hebrews 3:13 11) Hebrews 10:24
12) Romans 12:16, 17 13) Romans 15:7
14) Romans 13:8 15) Romans 14:13 16) I Peter 4:10
17) I Peter 5:5 18) Romans 12:14, 15 19) Colossians 3:13
20) I Peter 4:9 21) Galatians 6:2 22) Galatians 6:1
23) Ephesians 5:2 24) Galatians 6:3 25) Ephesians 5:21
26) James 5:16 27) Luke 17:3 28) Matthew 18:21,22
29) Ecclesiastes 7:8 30) Philippians 2:3
31) I Thessalonians 5:14*

CHAPTER 20

THE KEY OF ORGANIZATION

Let all things be done exactly and in order.[1]
Even the ants who are a people not strong,
prepare their meat in the summer.[2]

Well Known Biblical Examples:

1. Make thee an ark of gopher wood; rooms
shalt thou make in the ark, and shalt pitch it
within and without with pitch. And this is
the fashion which thou shalt make it of: the
length of the ark shall be three hundred
cubits, the breadth of it fifty cubits, and the
height of it thirty cubits. And of every living
thing of all flesh, two of every (sort) shalt
thou bring into the ark, to keep them alive
with thee; they shall be male and female.[3]

2. Moreover thou shalt provide out of all the
people able men, such as fear God, men of
truth, hating covetousness; and place such
over them, to be rulers of thousands, and
rulers of hundreds, rulers of fifties, and
rulers of tens: and Moses chose able men
out of all Israel, and made them heads over

the people, rulers of thousands, rulers of hundreds, rulers of fifties, and rulers of tens.[4]

3. In my Father's house are many mansions: if it were not so, I would have told you. I go to prepare a place for you; and if I go and prepare a place for you, I will come again, and receive you unto myself; that where I am, there ye may be also.[5]

4. And Solomon's builders and Hiram's builders did hew them, and the stonesquarers: so they prepared timber and stones to build the house.[6]

5. And David prepared iron in abundance for the nails for the doors of the gates, and for the joinings; and brass in abundance without weight; and David said, Solomon my son is young and tender, and the house that is to be builded for the LORD must be exceeding magnificent, of fame and of glory throughout all countries: I will therefore now make preparation for it. So David prepared abundantly before his death. Now behold, in my trouble I have prepared for the house of the LORD an hundred thousand talents of gold, and a thousand talents of silver, and the brass for things of brass, the iron for things of iron, and wood for things of wood; onyx stones, and stones to

be set, glistering stones, and of divers colors, and all manner of precious stones, and marble stones in abundance.[7]

6. According to all that I show thee, after the pattern of the tabernacle, and the pattern of all the instruments thereof, even so shall ye make it.[8]

7. In those days was Hezekiah sick unto death. And the prophet Isaiah the son of Amoz came to him, and said unto him, Thus saith the LORD, set thine house in order; for thou shalt die, and not live.[9]

References:

1) I Corinthians 14:40 2) Proverbs 30:25
3) Genesis 6:14–15, 19 4) Exodus 18:21, 25 5) John 14:2–3
6) I Kings 5:18 7) I Chronicles 22:3, 5, 14; 29:2
8) Exodus 25:9 9) II Kings 20:1

CHAPTER 21

THE KEY OF WISDOM

The fear of the Lord is the beginning of wisdom; and the knowledge of the Holy is understanding.[1] Incline your ear unto wisdom, apply your heart to understanding,[2] for wisdom is the principal thing,[3] far better than silver, gold[4] and rubies,[5] so with all thy getting[3] get wisdom[6] and understanding,[3] and forget it not.[6] Buy the truth, and sell it not; also wisdom, and instruction, and understanding,[7] not letting them depart from your eyes. Keep sound wisdom and discretion,[8] hear counsel and receive instruction, that you may be wise in the latter end.[9]

The tongue of the wise is health,[10] dispersing knowledge.[11] The words of a wise man are gracious,[12] like goads or nails firmly embedded,[13] and whereas a fool utters all his mind, a wise man keeps it in till afterwards.[14]

Wisdom is better than all things that may be compared to it.[15] It is better than weapons of war,[16] and strengthens the wise more than ten mighty men.[17] Through wisdom is a house built, and by understanding it is established.[18] When you find wisdom, there is a reward,[19] for wisdom is a defense,[20] making those who possess it strong.[21] The wise will be crowned with riches,[22] and inherit glory,[23] and have desired treasure and oil in their dwellings.[24]

If any of you lack wisdom, let him ask of God, that gives to all men liberally, without fault finding, and it shall be given him. But be sure to ask in faith, not doubting, for a double minded man is unstable in all his ways and won't receive anything from the Lord.[25] The wisdom from above is first of all pure, then peaceable, gentle, open to reason, full of mercy and good fruits, without partiality, and without hypocrisy.[26]

Wise men lay up knowledge,[27] and receive the commandments,[28] winning souls to the Lord.[29] When wisdom enters your heart, and knowledge is pleasant to your soul, discretion shall preserve you, and understanding will keep you.[30] Wisdom and prudence dwell together and find out knowledge of witty inventions.[31] The rod and reproof give wisdom,[32] and through desire a man, having separated himself seeks and intermeddles with all wisdom,[33] but in much wisdom is much grief, and he that increases knowledge, increases sorrow.[34]

Be wise as serpents and harmless as doves,[35] not wise in your own conceits,[36] for the wisdom of this world is foolishness with God.[37] If anyone among you seems to be wise in this world, let him become a fool, that he may be wise.[38] Become a fool for Christ's sake, and you will become wise in Christ[39] and have the very mind of Christ.[40]

God is made unto us wisdom, righteousness, sanctification and redemption.[41] Oh! the depth of the riches of the wisdom and knowledge of God.[42] So pray that you might be filled with the knowledge of His will in all wisdom and spiritual understanding,[43] knowing that in Christ are hid all the treasures of wisdom and knowledge.[44]

A wise man fears the Lord, shunning evil;[45] rebuke him, and he will love you for it.[46] In fact, give instruction to a wise man, and he will be yet wiser.[47] So walk with the wise, and you will be wise[48] and called prudent.[49] Then you will teach with your mouth[50] and feed many with your lips.[51]

Pride comes by contention,[52] and when pride comes, then comes shame: but with the lowly is wisdom,[53] and also with the well advised.[52] Even a fool, when he holds his peace, is counted wise; and he that shuts his lips is esteemed a man of understanding.[54]

For in the multitude of words, there wanteth not sin: but he that refrains his lips is wise.[55]

Finally, teach us to number our days, that we may apply our hearts unto wisdom.[56]

References:

1) Proverbs 9:10 2) Proverbs 2:2 3) Proverbs 4:7
4) Proverbs 16:16 5) Job 28:18 6) Proverbs 4:5
7) Proverbs 23:23 8) Proverbs 3:21 9) Proverbs 19:20
10) Proverbs 12:18 11) Proverbs 15:2
12) Ecclesiastes 10:12 13) Ecclesiastes 12:11
14) Proverbs 29:11 15) Proverbs 8:11
16) Ecclesiastes 9:18 17) Ecclesiastes 7:19
18) Proverbs 24:3 19) Proverbs 24:14 20) Ecclesiastes 7:12
21) Proverbs 24:5 22) Proverbs 14: 24 23) Proverbs 3:35
24) Proverbs 21:20 25) James 1:5-8 26) James 3:17
27) Proverbs 10:14 28) Proverbs 10:8 29) Proverbs 11:30
30) Proverbs 2:10-11 31) Proverbs 8:12 32) Proverbs 29:15
33) Proverbs 18:1 34) Ecclesiastes 1:18 35) Matthew 10:16
36) Romans 12:16 37) I Corinthians 3:19
38) I Corinthians 3:18 39) I Corinthians 4:10
40) I Corinthians 2:16 41) I Corinthians 1:30
42) Romans 11:33 43) Colossians 1:9 44) Colossians 2:3
45) Proverbs 14:16 46) Proverbs 9:8 47) Proverbs 9:9
48) Proverbs 13:20 49) Proverbs 16:21 50) Proverbs 16:23
51) Proverbs 10:21 52) Proverbs 13:10 53) Proverbs 11:2
54) Proverbs 17:28 55) Proverbs 10:19 56) Psalms 90:12

CHAPTER 22

THE KEY OF CONCENTRATION

Thou shalt love the Lord thy God with all thy heart, and with all thy soul, and with all thy mind, and with all thy strength: this is the first commandment.[1] And whatsoever you do, do it heartily as to the Lord and not unto men.[2]

Biblical Examples:

1. And Solomon determined to build a house for the name of the Lord, and a house for his kingdom.[3]

2. Then the disciples, every man according to his ability, determined to send relief unto the brethren which dwelt in Judea.[4]

3. For Paul had determined to sail by Ephesus, because he would not spend the time in Asia; for he hasted, if it were possible for him, to be at Jerusalem the day of Pentecost.[5] He also determined not to know anything among the Corinthians, except Jesus Christ, and Him crucified.[6]

4. Isaiah said, the Lord God will help me; therefore shall I not be confounded: I shall set my face like a flint, and I know that I shall not be ashamed.[7]

5. When King Hezekiah was deadly ill, he turned his face to the wall, and prayed unto the Lord.[8]

6. Then said he unto me, Fear not Daniel: for from the first day that you did set your heart to understand, and to chasten yourself before your God, your words were heard, and I am come for your words.[9]

7. And it came to pass, when the time was come for Jesus to be received up, He steadfastly set His face to go to Jerusalem.[10]

And Jesus said to them all, if any man will come after me, let him deny himself (lose sight of his own self interests and pursuits) and take up his cross daily, and follow me.[11]

With all your getting, get understanding,[12] and work for those over you with singleness of heart, as unto Christ.[13] Realize that you are not perfect, and do this one thing: forget those things which are behind, and reach forth to those things ahead, and press toward the mark for the prize of the high calling of God in Christ Jesus.[14]

Finally, brethren, whatsoever things are true, whatsoever things are honest, whatsoever things are just, whatsoever things are pure, whatsoever things are lovely, whatsoever things are of good report; if there be any virtue, and if there be any praise, fix your minds on these things.[15]

References:

1) Mark 12:30 2) Colossians 3:23 3) II Chronicles 2:1
4) Acts 11:29 5) Acts 20:16 6) I Corinthians 2:2
7) Isaiah 50:7 8) II Kings 20:2 9) Daniel 10:12
10) Luke 9:51 11) Luke 9:23 12) Proverbs 4:7
13) Ephesians 6:5 14) Philippians 3:13,14
15) Philippians 4:8

CHAPTER 23

THE KEY OF UNDERSTANDING AUTHORITY

Let every soul be subject unto the higher powers. For there is no power but of God; the powers that be are ordained of God. Whosoever therefore resists the power, resists the ordinance of God: and they that resist shall receive to themselves damnation. For rulers are not a terror to good works, but to the evil. Will you then not be afraid of the power? Do that which is good, and you shall have praise of the same. For he is the minister of God to you for good. But if you do that which is evil, be afraid; for he bears not the sword in vain; for he is the minister of God, a revenger to execute wrath upon him that does evil. Wherefore you must needs be subject, not only for wrath, but also for conscience sake.[1] I exhort therefore, that first of all, supplications, prayers, intercessions and giving of thanks, be made for all men; for kings and for all that are in authority; that we may lead a quiet and peaceable life in all godliness and honesty.[2] And remember to be subject to principalities and powers, to obey magistrates, to be ready for any honest work.[3]

Servants be subject to your masters with all

fear, not only to the good and gentle, but also to the harsh,[4] obeying them in all things, according to the flesh; not with eye service, as men pleasers, but in singleness of heart, fearing God,[5] pleasing them in all things not answering again.[6] You masters must understand that whatever good thing any man does, the same shall he receive of the Lord, whether he be bond or free. So forbear threatening,[7] give unto your servants that which is just and equally knowing that you also have a Master in heaven,[8] and there is no respect of persons with Him.[7]

When the righteous are in authority, the people rejoice; but when the wicked bears rule, the people mourn.[9] The hand of the diligent shall bear rule,[10] and a wise servant shall have rule over a son that causes shame.[11]

Remember them which have the rule over you, who have spoken unto you[12] the word of God, and obey them, submitting yourselves; for they watch over your souls, as they must give account,[13] whose faith follow, considering the end of their conversation.[12] Even so, every one of us shall give account of himself to God.[14]

He that has no rule over his own spirit is like a city that is broken down and without walls.[15] And if a man doesn't know how to rule his own house, how shall he take care of the church of God?[16] However, let the elders that rule well be counted worthy of double honor, especially they who labor in the word and doctrine.[17]

Christian servants should work hard for their masters, showing respect so as not to bring a reproach on the name of God.[18] If your master is a Christian, don't show them less respect because he is a brother, but rather, serve all the better, because those who benefit from their service are believers and beloved.[19]

God made man to have dominion over everything He made and put all things under his authority,[20] and those who have been faithful over little will be put in authority over much.[21]

References:

1) Romans 13:1-5 2) I Timothy 2:1, 2 3) Titus 3:1
4) I Peter 2:18 5) Colossians 3:22 6) Titus 2:9
7) Ephesians 6:8,9 8) Colossians 4:1 9) Proverbs 29:2
10) Proverbs 12:24 11) Proverbs 17:2 12) Hebrews 13:7
13) Hebrews 13:17 14) Romans 14:12 15) Proverbs 25:28
16) I Timothy 3:5 17) I Timothy 5:17 18) I Timothy 6:1
19) I Timothy 6:2 20) Psalms 8:6 21) Luke 19:17

CHAPTER 24

THE KEY OF TRAINING

Train up a child in the way he should go, and he will not depart from it.[1] Who can teach like God?[2] He even teaches my hands to war, so that a bow of steel is broken by my arms,[3] and He teaches my fingers to fight.[4] God will instruct you in discretion,[5] teach you how to profit,[6] teach you His paths and His ways,[7] guide the meek in judgement,[8] teach you His statutes,[9] good judgement and knowledge,[10] and even how to do His will;[11] only believe His commandments.[10]

The heart of the wise teaches his mouth, and adds learning to his lips.[12] Let God teach you to number your days that you may apply your heart to wisdom.[13] And when you don't know what to say, the Holy Ghost will teach you in the same hour what you ought to say.[14] But hear instruction, and be wise, refuse it not,[15] for he that refuses instruction despises his own soul; but he that hears reproof, gets understanding.[16] So apply your heart unto instruction and your ears to the words of knowledge,[17] for the commandment is a lamp; and the law is light; and reproofs of instruction are the way of life.[18] For you know that all scripture is given by inspiration of God, and is profitable for doctrine, for reproof, for correction, for instruction in righteousness, that the man of God may be perfect, thoroughly furnished unto all good works.[19]

Biblical Examples of Training:

1. And the LORD said unto Moses, Come up to me into the mount, and be there: and I will give thee tables of stone, and a law, and commandments which I have written; that thou mayest teach them.[20]

2. And you shall teach them diligently unto your children, and shall talk of them when you sit in your house, and when thou walk by the way, and when you lie down, and when you rise up.[21]

3. And when Abram heard that his brother was taken captive, he armed his trained servants, born in his own house, three hundred and eighteen, and pursued them unto Dan.[22]

Remember that the Lord will instruct you and teach you in the way you should go. He will guide you with His eye.[23] So learn to do well; seek judgement, relieve the oppressed, judge the fatherless, plead for the widow[24] and take the yoke upon you that Jesus offers, and learn of Him, for He is meek and lowly in heart; and you will find rest unto your soul.[25]

References:

1) Proverbs 22:6 2) Job 36:22 3) II Samuel 22:35
4) Psalms 144:1 5) Isaiah 28:26 6) Isaiah 48:17
7) Psalms 25:4 8) Psalms 25:9 9) Psalms 119:33
10) Psalms 119:66 11) Psalms 143:10 12) Proverbs 16:23
13) Psalms 90:12 14) Luke 12:12 15) Proverbs 8:33
16) Proverbs 15:32 17) Proverbs 23:12 18) Proverbs 6:23
19) II Timothy 3:16 20) Exodus 24:12
21) Deuteronomy 6:7 22) Genesis 14:14
23) Psalms 32:8 24) Isaiah 1:17 25) Matthew 11:29

CHAPTER 25

THE KEY OF TIME MANAGEMENT

Remember how short your time is,[1] and that to everything there is a season, and a time to every purpose under the heaven;[2] a time to be born, and a time to die; a time to plant, and a time to pluck up that which is planted; a time to kill, and a time to heal; a time to break down, and a time to build up; a time to weep, and a time to laugh; a time to mourn, and a time to dance; a time to cast away stones, and a time to gather stones together; a time to embrace, and a time to refrain from embracing; a time to get, and a time to lose; a time to keep, and a time to cast away; a time to rend, and a time to sew; a time to keep silence, and a time to speak; a time to love, and a time to hate; a time of war and a time of peace.[3] He has made everything beautiful in His time.[4] God shall judge the righteous and the wicked, for there is a time for every purpose and for every work.[5] Whoever keeps the commandment shall feel no evil thing; and a wise man's heart discerns both time and judgement, because to every purpose there is time and judgement.[6]

Walk in wisdom toward them that are without, redeeming the time,[7] because the days are evil.[8] Humble yourself therefore under the mighty hand of God, that He may exalt you in due time; casting all your care upon Him for He cares for you.[9] Watch therefore; for you know not what hour your Lord does come,[10] so be ready; for in such an hour as you think not, the Son of man will come.[11]

The hand of the diligent shall bear rule[12] and make rich.[13] His thoughts tend only to plenteousness,[14] and he knows the state of his flocks and condition of his herds.[15] He shall stand before kings, not just mean men,[16] and his soul shall be made fat.[17] The lazy, time waster on the other hand, shall be under tribute,[12] and poor,[13] desiring but having nothing,[17] for his hands refuse to labor.[18] So don't be slothful in business, but be fervent in spirit, serving the Lord.[19]

Ten Biblical Examples of God's Time Table:

1. But of that day and hour knoweth no man, no, not the angels of heaven, but my Father only. But as the days of Noah were, so shall also the coming of the Son of man be.[20]

2. For if you altogether hold your peace at

71

this time, then shall there enlargement and deliverance arise to the Jews from another place: but you and your father's house shall be destroyed: and who knows whether you are come to the kingdom for such a time as this?[21]

3. O that you would hide me in the grave, that you would keep me secret, until your wrath be past, that you would appoint me a set time, and remember me![22]

4. For this shall everyone that is godly pray unto you in a time when you may be found: surely in the floods of great waters they shall not come nigh unto him.[23]

5. But as for me, my prayer is unto you, O Lord, in an acceptable time: O God, in the multitude of your mercy hear me, in the truth of your salvation.[24]

6. Go ye up unto this feast: I go not up yet unto this feast: for my time is not yet fully come.[25]

7. For the vision is yet for an appointed time, but at the end it shall speak, and not lie; though it tarry, wait for it; because it will surely come, it will not tarry.[26]

8. Behold, I am against thee, O thou most

proud, saith the Lord God of hosts: for thy day is come, the time that I will visit thee.[27]

9. But when the time of the promise drew nigh, which God had sworn to Abraham, the people grew and multiplied in Egypt.[28]

10. Let both grow together until the harvest, and in the time of harvest I will say to the reapers, Gather ye together first the tares, and bind them in bundles to burn them: but gather the wheat into my barn.[29]

Time and chance happen to all,[30] but the time is short,[31] and you don't know what tomorrow holds. Even life itself is just a vapor, and then it vanishes away,[32] so let us not be weary in well doing, for in due season we shall reap, if we faint not.[33]

References:

1) Psalms 89:47 2) Ecclesiastes 3:1 3) Ecclesiastes 3:2-8
4) Ecclesiastes 3:11 5) Ecclesiastes 3:17 6) Ecclesiastes 8:5
7) Colossians 4:5 8) Ephesians 5:16 9) I Peter 5:6–7
10) Matthew 24:42 11) Matthew 24:44 12) Proverbs 12:24
13) Proverbs 10: 4 14) Proverbs 21:5 15) Proverbs 27:23
16) Proverbs 22:29 17) Proverbs 13:4 18) Proverbs 21:25
19) Romans 12:11 20) Matthew 24:36-37 21) Esther 4:14
22) Job 14:13 23) Psalms 32:6 24) Psalms 69:13
25) John 7:8 26) Habakkuk 2:3 27) Jeremiah 50:31
28) Acts 7:17 29) Matthew 13:30 30) Ecclesiastes 9:11
31) I Corinthians 7:29 32) James 4:14 33) Galatians 6:9

CHAPTER 26

THE KEY OF STRESS MANAGEMENT

Cast all your burdens[1] and cares[2] upon the Lord, for He cares for you, and He will sustain you. Yes, call upon the Lord in your day of distress, and He will hear you,[3] answer you,[4] redeem your soul,[5] set you in a large place[4] and bring you out of all your distresses.[6]

Listen to God. Let His peace rule in your heart,[7] and you shall dwell safely, free from fear of evil.[8] Don't allow your heart to be troubled or afraid[9] and be anxious for nothing, but in everything by prayer and supplication with thanksgiving let your requests be made known to God, and the peace of God which passes all understanding will keep your hearts and minds through Christ Jesus.[10] Remember that God will supply all your needs according to His riches in glory by Christ Jesus,[11] and He will keep you in perfect peace if your mind is fixed on Him.[12]

Don't give up, for God gives power to the

faint and to them that have no might, He increases strength.¹³ Wait upon the Lord to renew your strength, then you will mount up with wings as eagles, run and not be weary, walk and not faint.¹⁴ Make God your refuge and fortress,¹⁵ placing all your trust in Him¹⁶ and you will live in safety,¹⁷ preserved from trouble,¹⁸ surrounded by mercy,¹⁹ guarded by angels,²⁰ sheltered from the storm and shaded from the heat.²¹

God is our strength, a very present help in trouble.²² Call upon Him in the day of trouble, and He will come to your defense, be your refuge,²³ hide you in His pavilion,²⁴ set you upon a rock,²⁴ calm the storm and bring you to your desired haven.²⁵ During troubled times, He will be with you and honor you,²⁶ for His thoughts for you are precious, and great is the sum of them.²⁷ Remember that all things work together for good to them that love God, to them that are the called according to His purpose,²⁸ and He will perfect that which concerns you.²⁹

Jesus said, "Come unto me all ye that labor and are heavy laden, and I will give you rest. Take my yoke upon you, and learn of me; for I am meek and lowly in heart; and ye shall find rest unto your souls. For my yoke is easy and my burden is light.³⁰ Behold the fowls of the air; for they sow not, neither do they reap, nor gather into barns; yet your heavenly Father feedeth them. Are ye not much better than they? And why take ye thought for raiment? Consider the lilies of the field, how they grow; they toil not, neither do they spin: And yet I say unto you, that even Solomon in all his glory was not arrayed like one of these. Wherefore, if God so clothe the grass of the field, which today is and tomorrow is cast into the oven, shall He not much more clothe you, o ye of little faith? Take therefore no thought for the morrow: for the morrow shall take thought for the things of itself. Sufficient unto the day is the evil thereof."[31]

References:

1) Psalms 55:22 2) I Peter 5:7 3) Psalms 18:6
4) Psalms 118:5 5) I Kings 1:29 6) Psalms 107:28
7) Colossians 3:15 8) Proverbs 1:33 9) John 14:27
10) Philippians 4:6,7 11) Philippians 4:19
12) Isaiah 26:3 13) Isaiah 40:29 14) Isaiah 40:31
15) Psalm 91:2 16) Psalms 4:5 17) Psalms 4:8
18) Psalms 32:7 19) Psalms 32:10 20) Psalms 91:11
21) Isaiah 25:4 22) Psalms 46:1 23) Psalms 59:16
24) Psalms 27:5 25) Psalms 107:29,30 26) Psalms 91:15
27) Psalms 139:17 28) Romans 8:28 29) Psalms 138:8
30) Matthew 11:28-30 31) Matthew 6:26, 28-30,34

CHAPTER 27

THE KEY OF SETTING PRIORITIES

Seek ye first the kingdom of God, and His righteousness; and all these things shall be added unto you.[1] Follow Jesus first, and let the dead bury the dead.[2] And love the Lord your God with all your heart, with all your soul, and with all your mind, and with all your strength: this is the first commandment.[3] If any man comes to Christ, and hates not his father, and mother, and wife, and children, and brethren, and sisters, yes, his own life also, he cannot be His disciple. And whoever does not bear his own cross, and follow Jesus, cannot be his disciple.[4] So likewise, if any of you do not give up all that you have, you cannot be his disciple.[5]

First of all, supplications, prayers, intercessions, and giving of thanks should be made for all men.[6] For the time has come that judgement must begin at the house of God.[7] Therefore, we ought to give the more earnest heed to the things which we have heard, lest at any time we should let them slip.[8] So follow after charity, desire spiritual gifts,[9] depart from evil, seek peace and pursue it,[10] trust in the Lord and do good and you will dwell in the land, and verily you shall be fed.[11]

When entering a strong man's house to spoil his goods, you must first bind the strong man, then you can spoil his house.[12] When you bring your gift to the altar, if you remember that your brother has ought against you, leave your gift at the altar, and go first be reconciled to your brother, and then come and offer your gift.[13] When you notice a speck in your brother's eye, don't try and remove it until you first remove the log that is in your own eye.[14]

Those that love wisdom are loved of God, and those that seek wisdom early shall find it.[15] Awake early[16] and seek the Lord,[17] and if you seek Him with all your heart and soul, you will find Him.[18] Be kindly affectioned one to another with brotherly love; in honor preferring one another.[19] Know this, that many that are first shall be last, and the last shall be first.[20]

When the earth brings forth fruit of herself, you see first the blade, then the ear, and after that the full corn in the ear.[21] For precept must be upon precept, precept upon precept; line upon line, line upon line; here a little, and there a little.[22]

Be like Nehemiah who said, "I am doing a great work (rebuilding the wall) so I cannot come down and let the work cease."[23] Finally brethren, do this one thing, forget those things which are behind, reach forth to those things which are ahead, and press toward the mark for the prize of the high calling of God in Christ Jesus.[24]

References:

1) Matthew 6:33 2) Matthew 8:21,22 3) Mark 12:30
4) Luke 14:26, 27 5) Luke 14:33 6) I Timothy 2:1
7) I Peter 4:17 8) Hebrews 2:1 9) I Corinthians 14:1
10) Psalms 34:14 11) Psalms 37:3 12) Matthew 12:29
13) Matthew 5:23,24 14) Matthew 7:3-5 15) Proverbs 8:17
16) Psalms 57:8 17) Psalms 63:1 18) Deuteronomy 4:29
19) Romans 12:10 20) Matthew 19:30 21) Mark 4:28
22) Isaiah 28:10 23) Nehemiah 6:3
24) Philippians 3:13,14

CHAPTER 28

THE KEY OF DILIGENCE

Whatsoever is commanded by the God of heaven, let it be done diligently![1] He that diligently seeks good obtains favor,[2] and he that comes to God must believe that He is and that He is a rewarder of them that diligently seek Him.[3]

The hand of the diligent shall bear rule[4] and make rich, but the slack handed[5] slothful man shall be under tribute[4] and become poor.[5] The slothful[6] sluggardly man desires but has nothing,[7] and even what he took in hunting he won't bother to roast;[6] while the diligent man shall be made fat,[7] and his substance is precious.[6]

The thoughts of the diligent tend only to plenteousness; but of every one that is hasty only to want.[8] A diligent man knows the state of his flocks and condition of his herds,[9] and he will stand before kings, he shall not stand before mean men.[10]

And beside this, giving all diligence, add to your faith virtue; and to virtue, knowledge; and to knowledge, temperance; and to temperance, patience; and to patience, godliness; and to godliness, brotherly kindness; and to brotherly kindness, charity. For if these things be in you and abound, they make you so that you shall neither be barren nor unfruitful in the knowledge of our Lord Jesus Christ. Wherefore brethren, give diligence to make your calling and election sure: for if you do these things, you shall never fall.[11]

Remember to keep your heart with all diligence, for out of it are the issues of life.[12]

References:

1) Ezra 7:23 2) Proverbs 11:27 3) Hebrews 11:6
4) Proverbs 12:24 5) Proverbs 10:4 6) Proverbs 12:27
7) Proverbs 13:4 8) Proverbs 21:5 9) Proverbs 27:23
10) Proverbs 22:29 11) II Peter 1:5-8,10
12) Proverbs 4:23

CHAPTER 29

THE KEY OF OVERCOMING ADVERSITY

If you faint in the day of adversity, your strength is small.[1] You are of God and have overcome, because greater is He that is in you than he that is in the world.[2] For whatever is born of God, overcomes the world: and this is the victory that overcomes the world, even our faith. Who is he that overcomes the world, but he that believes that Jesus is the Son of God.[3]

Many are the afflictions of the righteous, but the Lord delivers him out of them all.[4] No man should be moved by afflictions,[5] rather endure them,[6] knowing that the same afflictions are accomplished in your brothers that are in the world.[7] Rejoice not against me, o my enemy: when I fall, I shall arise: when I sit in darkness, the Lord shall be a light unto me.[8] For a just man falls seven times, yet rises up again,[9] and I know that I can do all things through Christ who strengthens me.[10] Simply submit yourself to God. Resist the devil, and he will flee from you.[11] In this world, you will have tribulation; but be of good cheer; Jesus overcame the world,[12] so be not overcome with evil, but overcome evil with good.[13] and when you are in tribulation, if you turn to the Lord your God, and are obedient to His voice (for the Lord your God is a merciful God), He will not forsake you, neither destroy you, nor forget the covenant of your fathers which He sware unto them.[14]

He that has an ear, let him hear what the Spirit says to the churches; to him that overcomes will I give to eat of the tree of life, which is in the middle of the paradise of God,[15] and he will not be hurt of the second death.[16] I will give him to eat of the hidden manna and will give him a new name written, which no man knows except him that receives it.[17] I will give him power over the nations,[18] and not blot his name out of the book of life; instead I will confess his name before my Father, and before his angels.[19] Yes, he that overcomes will I make a pillar in the temple of my God, and he shall go no more out, and I will write upon him the name of my God, and the name of the city of my God, which is new Jerusalem, which comes down out of heaven from my God: and I will write upon him my new name.[20] I will grant him to sit with me in my throne, even as I also overcame, and am set down with my Father in his throne.[21] And he shall inherit all things; and I will be his God, and he shall be my son.[22]

Be patient in tribulation, continuing instant in prayer,[23] for tribulation works patience,[24] and besides, God comforts us in all our tribulation, that we may be able to comfort them which are in any trouble, by the comfort wherewith we ourselves are comforted of God.[25]

Remember that we are more than conquerors through Christ who loved us.[26] For I am persuaded that neither death, nor life, nor angels, nor principalities, nor powers, nor things present, nor things to come, nor height, nor depth, nor any other creature, shall be able to separate us from the love of God, which is in Christ Jesus our Lord.[27]

References:

*1) Proverbs 24:10 2) I John 4:4 3) I John 5:4, 5
4) Psalms 34:19 5) I Thessalonians 3:3 6) II Timothy 4:5
7) I Peter 5:9 8) Micah 7:8 9) Proverbs 24:16
10) Philippians 4:13 11) James 4:7 12) John 16:33
13) Romans 12:21 14) Deuteronomy 4:30,31
15) Revelation 2:7 16) Revelation 2:11
17) Revelation 2:17 18) Revelation 2:26 19) Revelation 3:5
20) Revelation 3:12 21) Revelation 3:21
22) Revelation 21:7 23) Romans 12:12 24) Romans 5:3
25) II Corinthians 1:4 26) Romans 8:37
27) Romans 8:38,39*

CHAPTER 30

THE KEY OF TRACKING RESULTS

Be diligent to know the state of your flocks, and look well to your herds,[1] not being slothful in business, but fervent in spirit; serving the Lord.[2]

Paul sent Timotheus to Philippi to know their state,[3] and Solomon managed a work force of 153,600 to get stone for the temple.[4] See the man that is diligent in his business? He shall stand before kings; he shall not stand before mean men.[5] The lord called his servant to him and asked him to give an account of his stewardship for he was about to lose his job.[6] So then, every one of us shall give account of himself to God.[7] But let a man examine himself[8] whether he be in the faith; and prove himself.[9]

References:

1) Proverbs 27:23 2) Romans 12:11 3) Philippians 2:19
4) II Chronicles 2:2 5) Proverbs 22:29 6) Luke 16:2
7) Romans 14:12 8) I Corinthians 11:28
9) II Corinthians 13:5

CHAPTER 31

THE KEY OF
VISION AND GOALS

And the Lord said, Write the vision, and
make it plain upon tables and billboards,
that he may run that reads it.[1] For where
there is no vision, the people perish;[2] but a
dream comes through the multitude of
business.[3]

God knows the desire of the humble; He will
prepare their heart and cause their ear to
hear.[4] For their desire is before God;[5] He
will give them their heart's desire and not
withhold the request of their lips.[6] Yes,
delight yourself in the Lord, and He will give
you the desires of your heart;[7] He will fulfill
the desire of them that fear Him. He will
also hear their cry and save them.[8]

The desire of the righteous is only good,[9]
and shall be granted,[10] and when it is
accomplished it is sweet to the soul.[11]
Through desire a man, having separated
himself, seeks and intermeddles with all
wisdom.[12]

Make the very most of time, seizing every opportunity, behaving wisely,[13] redeeming the time because the days are evil.[14] Buy the truth and sell it not; also wisdom, and instruction, and understanding.[15] Wherefore, be not unwise, but understanding what the will of the Lord is.[16]

Hope deferred makes the heart sick; but when the desire comes, it is a tree of life.[17] Forget those things which are behind, and reach forth to those things which are ahead, pressing toward the mark for the prize of the high calling of God in Christ Jesus.[18] And whatsoever things you desire when you pray, believe that you receive them and you shall have them.[19]

If a man desire the office of a bishop, he desires a good work.[20] So follow after love, and desire spiritual gifts, but rather that you may prophesy.[21] And if any man desire to be first, the same shall be last of all, and servant of all,[22] but desire the sincere milk of the word, that you may grow thereby.[23]

Notable Biblical Example of a Dream Fulfilled:

And it came to pass, when Solomon had finished the building of the house of the LORD, and the king's house, and all

Solomon's desire which he was pleased to do,...[24]

If a man knows to do good, and doesn't do it, to him it is sin.[25]

References:

1) Habakkuk 2:2 2) Proverbs 29:18 3) Ecclesiastes 5:3
4) Psalms 10:17 5) Psalms 38:9 6) Psalms 21:2
7) Psalms 37:4 8) Psalms 145:19 9) Proverbs 11:23
10) Proverbs 10:24 11) Proverbs 13:19 12) Proverbs 18:1
13) Colossians 4:5 14) Ephesians 5:16 15) Proverbs 23:23
16) Ephesians 5:17 17) Proverbs 13:12
18) Philippians 3:13,14 19) Mark 11:24 20) I Timothy 3:1
21) I Corinthians 14:1 22) Mark 9:35 23) I Peter 2:2
24) I King 9:1 25) James 4:17

CHAPTER 32

THE KEY OF PLANNING AND PREPARATION

For which of you, planning to build a tower, doesn't first sit down and count the cost, whether he has sufficient to finish it.[1] However, a man's heart plans his way, but the Lord directs his steps.[2] But when you have a vision, write it down, and make it plain, that those who see it can run with it.[3]

The preparation of the heart in man and the answer of the tongue is from the Lord.[4] Mercy and truth shall be to them that plan good.[5] Always be prepared to give an answer to every man that asks you a reason for the hope that is in you with meekness and fear.[6]

Biblical Examples of Planning and Preparation:

1. By faith Noah, being warned of God of things not seen as yet, moved with fear, prepared an ark to the saving of his house; by the which he condemned the world, and

became heir of the righteousness which is by faith.[7]

2. And David said, Solomon my son is young and tender, and the house that is to be builded for the LORD must be exceeding magnificent, of fame and of glory throughout all countries: I will therefore, now make preparation for it. So David prepared abundantly before his death.[8]

3. Even to prepare me timber in abundance: for the house which I am about to build shall be wonderful great.[9]

4. And David prepared iron in abundance for the nails for the doors of the gates, and for the joinings; and brass in abundance without weight. Now behold, in my trouble I have prepared for the house of the LORD an hundred thousand talents of gold, and a thousand talents of silver; and of brass and iron without weight; for it is in abundance: timber also and stone have I prepared; that thou mayest add thereto.

Now I have prepared with all my might for the house of my God the gold for things to be made of gold, and the silver for things of silver, and the brass for things of brass, the iron for things of iron, and wood for things of wood; onyx stones, and stones to be set, glistering stones, and of divers colors, and all manner of precious stones, and marble stones in abundance.[10]

5. Now the LORD had prepared a great fish to swallow up Jonah. And Jonah was in the belly of the fish three days and three nights.[11]

6. Then shall the King say unto them on his right hand, Come ye blessed of my Father, inherit the kingdom prepared for you from the foundation of the world...[12]

7. But as it is written, eye hath not seen, nor ear heard, neither have entered into the heart of man, the things which God hath prepared for them that love Him.[13]

8. And if I go and prepare a place for you, I will come again, and receive you unto myself; that where I am, there ye may be also.[14]

9. Thou preparest a table before me in the presence of mine enemies: thou anointest my head with oil; my cup runneth over.[15]

10. And next to him was Jehozabad, and with him an hundred and fourscore thousand ready prepared for the war.[16]

Final Reminder:

Now listen, you that say, today or tomorrow we will go into such a city, and continue there a year, and buy and sell, and get gain: whereas you know not what shall be on the morrow. For what is your life? It is even a vapor that appears for a little time, and then vanishes away. For that you ought to say, if the Lord will, we shall live, and do this or that.[17]

References:

1) Luke 14:28 2) Proverbs 16:9 3) Habakkuk 2:2
4) Proverbs 16:1 5) Proverbs 14:22 6) I Peter 3:15
7) Hebrews 11:7 8) I Chronicles 22:5
9) II Chronicles 2:9 10) I Chronicles 22:3,14 & 29:2
11) Jonah 1:17 12) Matthew 25:34 13) I Corinthians 2:9
14) John 14:3 15) Psalms 23:5 16) II Chronicles 17:18
17) James 4:13-15

CHAPTER 33

THE KEY OF TEAMWORK

Two are better than one, because they have a good reward for their labor. For if they fall, the one will lift up his fellow: but woe to him that is alone when he falleth; for he doesn't have another to help him up. Again if two lie together, then they have heat: but how can one be warm alone? And if one prevail against him, two shall withstand him; and a threefold cord is not easily broken.[1]

By the name of the Lord Jesus Christ, speak the same thing,[2] be like minded, having the same love, of one accord, of one mind,[3] and one mouth,[4] standing fast in one spirit, striving together for the faith of the gospel,[5] glorifying God,[4] living in peace and love,[6] perfectly joined together.[2] For we are laborers together with God: you are God's building,[7] in whom all the building fitly framed together grows unto a holy temple in the Lord: in whom you also are builded together for a habitation of God through the Spirit.[8]

For where two or three are gathered in Jesus' name, He is in the midst of them,[9] and what God hath joined together, let not man put asunder[10] And be not unequally yoked together with unbelievers: for what fellowship hath righteousness with unrighteousness? And what communion has light with darkness?[11]

Behold, how good and pleasant it is for brethren to dwell together in unity![12] Let's magnify the Lord and exalt His name together;[13] not forsaking the assembling of ourselves together, as the manner of some is; but exhorting one another: and so much the more as you see the day approaching;[14] that your hearts might be comforted, being knit together in love, and unto all riches of the full assurance of understanding, to the acknowledgement of the mystery of God, and of the Father, and of Christ:[15] knowing that the whole body is fitly joined together and compacted by that which every joint supplieth, according to the effectual working in the measure of every part, makes increase of the body unto the edifying of itself in love.[16]

Biblical Examples:

1. So built we the wall; and all the wall was joined together unto the half thereof; for the people had a mind to work.[17]

2. And the Lord said, Behold, the people is one, and they have all one language; and

this they begin to do: and now nothing will be restrained from them, which they have imagined to do.[18]

3. And when the day of Pentecost was fully come, they were all with one accord in one place.[19]

Finally, be ye all of one mind, having compassion one of another, love as brethren, be pitiful and be courteous,[20] endeavoring to keep the unity of the Spirit in the bond of peace.[21]

References:

1) Ecclesiastes 4:9-12 2) I Corinthians 1:10
3) Philippians 2:2 4) Romans 15:6 5) Philippians 1:27
6) II Corinthians 13:11 7) I Corinthians 3:9
8) Ephesians 2:21, 22 9) Matthew 18:20 10) Mark 10:9
11) II Corinthians 6:14 12) Psalms 133:1 13) Psalms 34:3
14) Hebrews 10:25 15) Colossians 2:2 16) Ephesians 4:16
17) Nehemiah 4:6 18) Genesis 11:6 19) Acts 2:1
20) I Peter 3:8 21) Ephesians 4:3

CHAPTER 34

THE KEY OF BREAKTHROUGH IDEAS

Wisdom dwells with prudence and finds out knowledge of witty inventions.[1] For the Lord gives[2] and lays up sound wisdom for the righteous.[3] Out of His mouth comes knowledge and understanding,[2] and He is a buckler to them that walk uprightly.[3] The fear of the Lord is the beginning of wisdom, the knowledge of the Holy is understanding,[4] and a good understanding have all they that do His commandments.[5] Through desire a man, having separated himself, seeketh and intermeddleth with all wisdom,[6] and through wisdom is a house built, and by understanding it is established.[7]

Wait on the Lord, and He shall lead you in truth, and teach you,[8] yes He will instruct you and teach you in the way you should go and guide you with His eye.[9] It is the Lord your God which teaches you to profit and leads you where you should go.[10] Call unto God and He will answer you and show you great and mighty things, which you know not,[11] for God is a God of gods, and a Lord of kings, and a revealer of secrets.[12] And it's true, the secret of the Lord is with them that fear Him.[13]

There is a spirit in man, and the inspiration of the Almighty gives him understanding.[14] But we have the mind of Christ,[15] and the Father of glory gives unto us the spirit of wisdom and revelation in the knowledge of Jesus Christ.[16] Yes the Spirit searches all things, yes, the deep things of God,[17] and He reveals the deep and secret things, for He knows what is in the darkness, and the light dwells with Him.[18] Surely the Lord God will do nothing, but he revealeth his secret unto his servants the prophets.[19]

Biblical Examples:

1. Then was the secret revealed unto Daniel in a night vision.[20]

2. And Uzziah made in Jerusalem engines, invented by cunning men, to be on the towers and upon the bulwarks, to shoot arrows and great stones. And his name spread far abroad; for he was marvelously helped, till he was strong.[21]

3. Let them make Me a sanctuary, that I may dwell among them, and you (Moses) shall do according to all that I show you, after the

pattern of the tabernacle.[22]

4. And call Jesse to the sacrifice, and I will show you what you should do.[23]

5. How that by revelation, He made known unto me (Paul) the mystery.[24]

References:

1) Proverbs 8:12 2) Proverbs 2:6 3) Proverbs 2:7
4) Proverbs 9:10 5) Psalms 111:10 6) Proverbs 18:1
7) Proverbs 24:3 8) Psalms 25:5 9) Psalms 32:8
10) Isaiah 48:17 11) Jeremiah 33:3 12) Daniel 2:47
13) Psalms 25:14 14) Job 32:8 15) I Corinthians 2:16
16) Ephesians 1:17 17) I Corinthians 2:10
18) Daniel 2:22 19) Amos 3:7 20) Daniel 2:19
21) II Chronicles 26:15 22) Exodus 25:8,9
23) I Samuel 16:3 24) Ephesians 3:3

CHAPTER 35

THE KEY OF IDENTIFYING LEADERSHIP QUALITIES

The Lord sees not as man sees; for man looks on the outward appearance, but the Lord looks on the heart[1] and has set him aside that is godly for Himself.[2] God chooses men of honest report, full of the Holy Ghost and wisdom, to appoint over certain business.[3] But notice brethren, how that not many wise men after the flesh, not many mighty, not many noble, are called: but God has chosen the foolish things of the world to confound the wise; and God has chosen the weak things of the world to confound the things which are mighty; and base things of the world, and things which are despised, has God chosen, yes, and things which are not, to bring to nought things that are: that no flesh should glory in His presence.[4]

God looks favorably on a just man who fears God and of a good report,[5] full of the Holy Ghost and faith,[6] but especially looks for a man after His own heart.[7] All elders who rule well should be counted worthy of double honor, especially they who labor in the word and doctrine.[8]

Qualifications For a Bishop:

This is a true saying, if a man desire the office of a bishop, he desireth a good work. A bishop then must be blameless, the husband of one wife, vigilant, sober, of good behavior, given to hospitality, apt to teach; not given to wine, no striker, not greedy of filthy lucre; but patient, not a brawler, not covetous; one that ruleth well his own house, having his children in subjection with all gravity; for if a man know not how to rule his own house, how shall he take care of the church of God? Not a novice, lest being lifted up with pride he fall into the condemnation of the devil. Moreover, he must have a good report of them which are without; lest he fall into reproach and the snare of the devil. Likewise, must the deacons be grave, not double tongued, not given to much wine, not greedy of filthy lucre; holding the mystery of the faith in a pure conscience. And let these also first be proved; then let them use the office of a deacon, being found blameless. Even so must their wives be grave, not slanderers, sober, faithful in all things. Let the deacons be the husband of one wife, ruling their children and their own houses well.

For they that have used the office of a deacon well purchase to themselves a good degree, and great boldness in the faith which is in Christ Jesus.[9]

Abraham believed God, and it was imputed to him for righteousness[10] and through wisdom,[11] the hand of the diligent shall bear rule.[12]

References:

1) I Samuel 16:7 2) Psalms 4:3 3) Acts 6:3
4) I Corinthians 1:26-29 5) Acts 10:22 6) Acts 11:24
7) I Samuel 13:14 8) I Timothy 5:17 9) I Timothy 3:1-13
10) James 2:23 11) Proverbs 8:16 12) Proverbs 12:24

CHAPTER 36

THE KEY OF BENEFICIAL ASSOCIATIONS

He that walks with wise men shall be wise: but a companion of fools shall be destroyed,[1] and he that keeps company with harlots spends all his substance.[2] Have no fellowship with the unfruitful works of darkness, but rather reprove them.[3]

Don't be unequally yoked together with unbelievers: for what fellowship has righteousness with unrighteousness? And what communion has light with darkness?[4] But if we walk in the light, we have fellowship one with another, and the blood of Jesus Christ His Son cleanses us from all sin.[5]

You adulterers and adulteresses, don't you know that the friendship of the world is enmity with God? Whosoever therefore will be a friend of the world is the enemy of God.[6] Don't keep company with any man that is called a Christian if he is a fornicator, or covetous, or an idolater, or a railer, or a drunkard, or an extortioner; with such a one, don't even eat.[7]

Blessed is the man that walks not in the counsel of the ungodly, nor stands in the way of the sinners, nor sits in the seat of the scornful. But his delight is in the law of the Lord; and in His law he meditates day and night. He shall be like a tree planted by the rivers of water, that brings forth fruit in its season; his leaf also shall not wither; and whatsoever he does shall prosper.[8]

A wise man will hear and will increase learning; and a man of understanding shall attain unto wise counsels.[9]

References:

*1) Proverbs 13:20   2) Proverbs 29:3   3) Ephesians 5:11
4) II Corinthians 6:14   5) I John 1:7   6) James 4:4
7) I Corinthians 5:11   8) Psalms 1:1-3   9) Proverbs 1:5*

CHAPTER 37

THE KEY OF UNDERSTANDING LEGAL MATTERS AND CONTRACTS

God said, My covenant will I not break nor alter the thing which is gone out of My lips.[1] If a man vow a vow unto the LORD, or swear an oath to bind his soul with a bond; he shall not break his word, but he shall do according to all that proceeds out of his mouth.[2] When you vow a vow unto God, defer not to pay it; for He has no pleasure in fools; pay that which you have vowed.[3] It is better that you should not vow, than to vow and not pay.[4]

Let none of you imagine evil in your hearts against your neighbor; and love no false oath; for all these are things God hates;[5] but above all things, my brethren, swear not, neither by heaven, neither by the earth, neither by any other oath; but let your yea be yea, and your nay, nay; lest you fall into condemnation.[6] You are snared with the words of your mouth and taken by them.[7] Again, you have heard that it has been said by them of old time, thou shalt not forswear thyself, but shalt perform unto the Lord thine oaths; but I say unto you, swear not at all; neither by heaven, for it is God's throne; nor by the earth, for it is His footstool; neither by Jerusalem, for it is the city of the great King. Neither shall you swear by your head, because you cannot make one hair white or black. But let your communication be yea, yea; nay, nay; for whatsoever is more than these cometh of evil.[8]

Biblical Examples of Contracts:

1. Send me now therefore a man cunning to work in gold, and in silver, and in brass, and in iron, and in purple, and crimson, and blue, and that can skill to grave with the cunning men that are with me in Judah and in Jerusalem, whom David my father did provide. Send me also cedar trees, fir trees, and algum trees, out of Lebanon: for I know that thy servants can skill to cut timber in Lebanon; and, behold, my servants shall be with thy servants, even to prepare me timber in abundance: for the house which I am about to build shall be wonderful great. And, behold, I will give to thy servants, the hewers that cut timber, twenty thousand measures of beaten wheat, and twenty thousand measures of barley, and twenty thousand baths of wine, and twenty thousand

baths of oil. Then Hiram the king of Tyre answered in writing, which he sent to Solomon, Because the LORD hath loved His people, he hath made thee king over them.[9]

2. Now in the first year of Cyrus king of Persia, that the word of the LORD spoken by the mouth of Jeremiah m:ght be accomplished, the LORD stirred up the spirit of Cyrus king of Persia, that he made a proclamation throughout all his kingdom, and put it also in writing, saying . . .[10]

3. And because of all this we make a sure covenant, and write it, and our princes, Levites, and priest, seal unto it.[11]

A Reminder:

Be not unequally yoked together with unbelievers; for what fellowship has righteousness with unrighteousness? And what communion has light with darkness?[12]

Dare any of you, having a matter against another, go to law before the unjust, and not before the saints? Do ye not know that the saints shall judge the world? And if the world shall be judged by you, are you unworthy to judge the smallest matters? Don't you know that we shall judge angels?

How much more things that pertain to this life? If then you have judgements of things pertaining to this life, set them to judge who are least esteemed in the church. I speak to your shame, Is it so, that there is not a wise man among you? No not one that shall be able to judge between his brethren? But brother goeth to law with brother, and that before the unbelievers. Now therefore there is utterly a fault among you, because you go to law one with another. Why do you not rather take wrong? Why do you not rather suffer yourselves to be defrauded? Nay, you do wrong, and defraud, and that your brother.[13] And if any man will sue you at the law, and take away your coat, let him have your cloak also.[14]

Therefore, if you bring your gift to the altar, and there remember that your brother has ought against you, leave there your gift before the altar, and go your way; first be reconciled to your brother, and then come and offer your gift. Agree with your adversary quickly, while you are in the way with him; lest at any time the adversary deliver you to the judge, and the judge deliver you to the officer, and you be cast into prison. Verily, I say unto you, you shall by no means come out until you have paid the uttermost farthing.[15] But I say unto you, that whoever is angry with his brother without cause shall be in danger of the judgement.[16] Rather, love your enemies, bless them that curse you, do good to them that hate you, and pray for them which despitefully use you and persecute you.[17] For if you forgive men their trespasses, your heavenly Father will also forgive you, but if you forgive not men their trespasses, neither will your Father forgive your trespasses.[18]

References:

1) Psalms 89:34 2) Numbers 30:2 3) Ecclesiates 5:4
4) Ecclesiastes 5:5 5) Zechariah 8:17 6) James 5:12
7) Proverbs 6:2 8) Matthew 5:33-37
9) II Chronicles 2: 7-11 10) II Chronicles 36:22
11) Nehemiah 9:38 12) II Corinthians 6:14
13) I Corinthians 6:1–8 14) Matthew 5:40
15) Matthew 5:23-26 16) Matthew 5:22
17) Matthew 5:44 18) Matthew 6: 14–15

CHAPTER 38

THE KEY OF ADVERTISING

A good name is rather to be chosen than great riches[1] or precious ointment,[2] and loving favor rather than silver and gold.[1] Dead flies will cause even perfume to stink, so a small mistake can hurt a man's reputation for wisdom and honor.[3]

Wait on the Lord;[4] keep His way and exalt His wisdom,[5] and He shall exalt you to inherit the land,[4] and by embracing His wisdom you will be brought to honor.[5] For promotion comes neither from the east, nor the west, nor from the south, but God is the judge: He putteth one down and setteth up another.[6] It is better to let another man praise you instead of your own mouth; a stranger instead of your own lips.[7] When Jesus healed a leper the man began to publish it much, and to blaze abroad the matter, insomuch that Jesus could no more openly enter into the city, but was out in desert places: and they came to Him from every quarter.[8]

The psalmist said, "My tongue is the pen of a ready writer."[9] God told Habakkuk to write the vision on a billboard, make it large and clear so that anyone can read it and rush to tell others about it.[10] Most men will proclaim every one his own goodness: but a faithful man is hard to find.[11]

A good report makes the bones fat![12]

References:

1) Proverbs 22:1 2) Ecclesiastes 7:1 3) Ecclesiastes 10:1
4) Psalms 37:34 5) Proverbs 4:8 6) Psalms 75:6,7
7) Proverbs 27:2 8) Mark 1:45 9) Psalms 45:1
10) Habakkuk 2:2 11) Proverbs 20:6 12) Proverbs 15:30

CHAPTER 39

STEWARDSHIP

The Lord will choose a faithful and wise steward to make ruler over his household, to give them their portion of meat in due season.[1] The Lord even commended the unjust steward for he had done wisely: for the children of this world are in their generation wiser than the children of light.[2] Joseph found grace in Potiphar's sight, and he served him: and he made him overseer over his house, and all that he had put into his hand. And it came to pass from the time that he had made him overseer in his house, and over all that he had, that the Lord blessed the Egyptians's house for Joseph's sake.[3]

When the faithful servant had doubled his lord's money, the lord said unto him, Well done good and faithful servant; you have been faithful over a few things, I will make thee ruler over many things: enter thou into the joy of the Lord.[4]

Now there are diversities of gifts, but the same Spirit. And there are differences of administrations, but the same Lord.[5] Having then gifts differing according to the grace that is given to us, whether prophecy, let us prophesy according to the proportion of faith; or ministry, let us wait on our ministering: or he that teacheth, on teaching: or he that exhorteth, on exhortation; he that giveth, let him do it with simplicity; he that showeth mercy, with cheerfulness.[6]

Now concerning the collection for the saints, as I have given order to the churches of Galatia, you do also. Upon the first day of the week let every one of you lay by him in store, as God has prospered him.[7]

References:

1) Luke 12:42 2) Luke 16:8 3) Genesis 39:4,5
4) Matthew 25:22,23 5) I Corinthians 12:4,5
6) Romans 12:6-8 7) I Corinthinans 16:1,2

CHAPTER 40

BORROWING, LENDING AND DEBT

Owe no man anything, but to love one another,[1] for the rich ruleth over the poor, and the borrower is servant to the lender.[2] The wicked borrows and doesn't pay back; but the righteous show mercy and give.[3] He that has pity upon the poor, lends unto the Lord; and that which he has given will he pay him again.[4] But love your enemies and do good, and lend, hoping for nothing again; and your reward shall be great, and you shall be the children of the Highest: for He is kind unto the unthankful and to the evil.[5]

Give to him that asks of thee, and from him that would borrow from you, turn not away.[6] And if a man borrow ought of his neighbor, and it gets damaged, or dies, without its owner being with it, the borrower shall make full restitution.[7] Withhold not good from those to whom it is due, when it is your power to do it.[8]

The righteous is ever merciful, and lendeth;

and his seed is blessed,[9] yes a good man shows favor, and lends; he will guide his affairs with discretion.[10] Those in covenant relationship with the Lord will lend unto many nations and not borrow.[11]

If you lend money to any of God's people who are poor you shall not be a creditor to him and you shall not require interest of him.[12] In fact, if your brother be poor and unable to support himself, let him live with you awhile as a guest. Fear God and let him stay with you and don't charge him interest on the money you lend him. You must not lend him money at interest or sell him food for a profit.[13] If there be a poor man of one of your brethren in any of the towns in the land which the Lord your God gives you, don't harden your heart, nor shut your hand from this poor brother, but open your hand wide unto him and lend him sufficient for his need, in that which he wants.[14]

Do not charge your brother interest on money or food or anything else. You may charge a foreigner interest but not your brother, that the Lord your God may bless you in everything you set your hand to in the land you are entering to possess.[15]

If you lend anything to another man, do not go inside his house to get his security for the loan. Wait outside and the owner to whom you are lending the money will bring it to you. If the man is poor and gives you his cloak for security, do not sleep in it. Return his cloak to him by sundown so that he may sleep in it. Then he will bless you and it will be counted righteousness unto you before the Lord your God.[16]

References:

1) Romans 13:8 2) Proverbs 22:7 3) Psalms 37:21
4) Proverbs 19:17 5) Luke 6:35 6) Matthew 5:42
7) Exodus 22:14 8) Proverbs 3:27 9) Psalms 37:26
10) Psalms 112:5 11) Deuteronomy 28:12
12) Exodus 22:25 13) Leviticus 25:35–36
14) Deuteronomy 15:7–8 15) Deuteronomy 23: 19–20
16) Deuteronomy 24:10-13

CHAPTER 41

CO-SIGNING

Be not one of them that strike hands, or of them that are sureties for debts, for if you have nothing with which to pay, why should your bed be taken from you?[1]

A man void of understanding strikes hands, and becomes surety in the presence of his friend,[2] and if he is surety for a stranger, he shall suffer for it; and he that hates suretyship is safe and secure.[3]

My son, if you are surety for your friend, if you have struck hands with a stranger, you are snared with the words of your mouth, yes you are taken with the words of your mouth. Do this now, my son, and deliver yourself, for you have come into your neighbor's power; go humble yourself, plead with your neighbor; give not sleep to your eyes, nor slumber to your eyelids. Deliver yourself as a roe from the hand of a hunter, and as a bird from the hand of the fowler.[4]

References:

1) Proverbs 22:26,27 2) Proverbs 17:18
3) Proverbs 11:15 4) Proverbs 6:1-5

CHAPTER 42

THE INFLUENCE OF MONEY

Wealth makes many friends; but the poor is separated from his neighbor.[1] The poor uses entreaties,[2] and is hated even of his own neighbor, but the rich has many friends,[3] and answers roughly.[2] The ransom of a man's life are his riches; but the poor heareth not rebuke.[4]

For wisdom is a defense and money is a defense; but the excellency of knowledge is that wisdom gives life to them that have it.[5]

For the love of money is the root of all evil: which while some coveted after, they have erred from the faith, and pierced themselves through with many sorrows.[6]

And remember, the rich ruleth over the poor, and the borrower is servant to the lender.[7]

References:

1) Proverbs 19:4   2) Proverbs 18:23   3) Proverbs 14:20
4) Proverbs 13:8   5) Ecclesiastes 7:12
6) I Timothy 6:10   7) Proverbs 22:7

CHAPTER 43

GIVING AND RECEIVING

Blessed is he that considers the poor[1] and has pity on them, for he lends unto the Lord; and that which he has given will he pay him again,[2] and the Lord will deliver him in the day of trouble.[1] There is that makes himself rich, yet has nothing; there is that makes himself poor, yet has great riches.[3] It is a sore evil when riches are kept just for the owners, to their own hurt.[4] So charge them that are rich in this world, that they be not highminded, nor trust in uncertain riches; but in the living God, who gives us richly all things to enjoy;[5] that they do good, that they may be rich in good works, ready to distribute, willing to communicate laying up in store for themselves a good foundation against the time to come, that they may lay hold on eternal life.[6] For they that be rich fall into temptation and a snare, and into many foolish and hurtful lusts, which draw men in destruction and perdition.[7] So remember that as surely as the grass withers and the flower falls, so also the rich man will fade away in his ways.[8]

Lay not up for yourselves treasures upon

earth, where moth and rust does corrupt, and where thieves break through and steal; but lay up for yourselves treasures in heaven, where neither moth nor rust does corrupt, and where thieves do not break through and steal: for where your treasure is, there will your heart be also.**⁹** If you be risen with Christ, seek those things which are above, where Christ sits on the right hand of God. Set your affection on things above, not on things on the earth.**¹⁰**

No man can serve two masters; for either he will hate the one, and love the other; or else he will hold to the one, and despise the other. You cannot serve God and money. Therefore, take no thought for your life, what you shall eat, or what you shall drink; nor yet for your body, what you shall put on. Is not the life more than meat, and the body than raiment? Behold the fowls of the air; for they sow not, neither do they reap, nor gather into barns; yet your heavenly Father feedeth them. Are you not much better than they? Which of you by taking thought can add one cubit unto his stature? And why take thought for raiment? Consider the lilies of the field, how they grow; they toil not, neither do they spin; And yet I say unto you, that even Solomon in all his glory was not arrayed like one of these. Wherefore, if God so clothe the grass of the field, which today is, and tomorrow is cast into the oven, shall He not much more clothe you, o ye of little faith? Therefore, take no thought, saying, what shall we eat? or what shall we drink? or wherewithal shall we be clothed? For after all these things do the Gentiles seek: for your heavenly Father knows that you have need of all these things. But seek ye first the kingdom of God, and His righteousness; and all these things shall be added unto you. Take therefore no thought for the morrow; for the morrow shall take thought for the things of itself. Sufficient unto the day is the evil thereof.[11]

Give to him that asks of you, and from him that would borrow from you, turn not away.[12] For what man is there of you, whom if his son ask bread, will he give him a stone? Or if he ask for a fish, will he give him a serpent? If you, being evil, know how to give good gifts to your children, how much more shall your Father which is in heaven, give good things to them that ask him?[13] Freely you have received, freely give.[14] Yes, give and it shall be given unto you; good measure, pressed down, shaken together, and running over shall men give into your bosom. For the same measure you give will be the measure you get back.[15] But let everyone give as he has decided in his heart, not grudgingly or under compulsion; for God loves a cheerful giver.[16]

Let him that stole, steal no more; but rather let him labor, working with his hands the thing which is good, that he may have to give to him that needs.[17] When someone in need comes to you, don't say, "Depart in peace, be warmed and filled," and then not give them what they need for their body, for what good is that?[18]

There is no one that has left houses or brothers or sisters or father or mother or wife or children or lands, for Jesus' sake and the gospel's, but that he shall receive a hundredfold now in this time houses, and brothers and sisters and mothers and children and lands with persecutions; and in the world to come eternal life.[19] Remember that a man's life does not consist of the abundance of things which he possesses.[20]

Honor the Lord with your substance, and with the firstfruits of all your increase, so shall your barns be filled with plenty, and your presses shall burst out with new wine.[21] And remember, God is able to do exceeding abundantly above all that we ask or think, according to the power that works in us,[22] for eye has not seen, nor ear heard, neither have entered into the heart of man, the things

which God has prepared for them that
love Him.[23]

References:

1) Psalms 41:1 2) Proverbs 19:17 3) Proverbs 13:7
4) Ecclesiastes 5:13 5) I Timothy 6:17
6) I Timothy 6:18-19 7) I Timothy 6:9 8) James 1:11
9) Matthew 6:19-21 10) Colossians 3:1
11) Matthew 6: 24-34 12) Matthew 5:42
13) Matthew 7:9-11 14) Matthew 10:8 15) Luke 6:38
16) II Corinthians 9:7 17) Ephesians 4:28
18) James 2:16 19) Mark 10:29-30 20) Luke 12:15
21) Proverbs 3: 9-10 22) Ephesians 3:20
23) I Corinthians 2:9

CHAPTER 44

TITHING

Will a man rob God? Yet you have robbed God; but you say, how have we robbed Him? In tithes and offerings! You are cursed with a curse: for you have robbed God, even the whole nation. Bring all your tithes into the storehouse, that there may be meat in God's house, and prove God with this, if He will not open for you, the windows of heaven and pour you out a blessing that there shall not be room enough to receive it. And God will rebuke the devourer for your sake, and He will not destroy the fruit of your ground; neither shall your vine cast her fruit before the time in the field.[1]

All of the tithe of the land, whether of the seed of the land, or of the fruit of the tree, is the Lord's; it is holy unto the Lord.[2] You shall truly tithe all the increase of your seed, that the field brings forth year by year.[3] When Melchizedek, king of Salem, met with Abram, he blessed him saying, Blessed be Abram of the most high God, possessor of heaven and earth; and blessed be the most high God, which has delivered your enemies into your hand. Then Abram gave him tithes of all.[4]

But woe unto you Pharisees, for you tithe of even the smallest part of your income, but you neglect the justice and love of God. You should have practiced the latter without leaving the former undone.[5]

References:

1) Malachi 3:8-11 2) Leviticus 27:30 3) Deuteronomy 14:22
4) Genesis 14:19-20 5) Luke 11:42

CHAPTER 45

PROSPERITY

Let the Lord be magnified which has pleasure in the prosperity of His servant.[1] Only be strong and very courageous, that you may observe to do according to all the law, and turn not from it to the right hand or the left, that you may prosper wherever you go.[2] Yes, keep the words of His covenant,[3] walk in His ways, keeping His statutes, commandments, judgments and testimonies[4] and these blessings will come upon you and overtake you. You will be blessed in the city and field, in the fruit of your body, and the fruit of your ground, the fruit of your cattle, and all your flocks and herds. Your basket and storehouse will be blessed, when you're coming and going, and God will command a blessing upon you in your storehouse and in all you set your hand to. The Lord will open up His good treasure to you, and you will lend to many nations and not borrow. He will make you the head and not the tail, above only and not beneath, prospering wherever you go,[5] if you hearken unto the commandments of the Lord your God, to observe and to do them.[6]

The blessing of the Lord makes rich, and He

adds no sorrow with it,[7] so labor not to be rich and cease from your own wisdom,[8] for he that is hasty to be rich has an evil eye and considers not that poverty will come upon him.[9] In fact by humility and the fear of the Lord, are riches and honor and life.[10]

Blessings are upon the head of the just,[11] and a faithful man will abound with them.[12] In the house of the wise[13] and righteous is much treasure[14] to be desired, and oil.[13] Wealth gotten hastily[12] or with vanity shall diminish[15] and those who do so[12] or oppress the poor to increase riches[16] shall not be innocent[12] and will come to want.[16]

Riches are not forever;[17] they even make themselves wings and fly away like an eagle towards heaven,[18] and he that trusts in them shall fall.[19] Seek after wisdom, for length of days is in her right hand and in her left hand are riches and honor;[20] yes durable riches and righteousness.[21] Those that love wisdom, and seek her early will find her,[22] for she leads in the way of righteousness, in the midst of the paths of judgement,[23] that she may cause you to inherit substance, and she will fill your treasures.[24]

Strong men retain riches,[25] but they will not profit in the day of wrath.[26] He that loves pleasure will be a poor man, and he that loves wine and oil shall not be rich.[27] But the thoughts of the diligent tend only to plenteousness,[28] and he that tills his land shall have plenty of bread.[29] Yes, the hand of the diligent makes rich, but he that deals with a slack hand becomes poor.[30]

By knowledge shall the chambers be filled with all precious and pleasant riches.[31] For you know the grace of our Lord Jesus Christ, that though He was rich, yet for your sakes He became poor, that you through His poverty might be rich.[32] Did you know that the wealth of the sinner is laid up for the just?[33] For God gives to a man that is good in His sight wisdom, and knowledge, and joy; but to the sinner He gives work, to gather and to heap up, that he may give to him that is good before God.[34] So remember the Lord your God, for it is He that gives you power to get wealth, that he may establish His covenant, which He sware unto your fathers, as it is this day.[35]

Praise the Lord. Blessed is the man that fears the Lord, that delights greatly in His commandments. His seed shall be mighty upon the earth; the generation of the upright shall be blessed. Wealth and riches shall be in his house: and his righteousness endures forever.[36] It is the gift of God for a man to have riches and wealth, to be able to eat and take his portion and to rejoice in his labor.[37]

God has spoken, you are called of God, He has brought you and He will make your way prosperous,[38] for salvation belongs to the Lord and His blessing is upon His people.[39] Yes, even the blessing of Abraham, which came upon the Gentiles through Jesus Christ.[40]

The Lord said "In blessing, I will bless you and in multiplying, I will multiply you";[41] nevertheless I call heaven and earth to record this day against you, that I have set before you life and death, blessing and cursing; therefore, choose life, that both you and your seed may live."[42]

A good name is rather to be chosen than great riches, and loving favor rather than silver and gold,[4] but if riches increase, set not your heart upon them.[44] Remember the Lord makes poor, and makes rich; He brings low and lifts up,[45] knowing that it is difficult for those with riches to enter into the kingdom of God.[46] So let no man seek his own, but every man, another's wealth.[47]

Blessed is the man that walks not in the counsel of the ungodly, nor stands in the way of the sinner, nor sits in the seat of the scornful. But his delight is in the law of the Lord and in His law does he meditate day and night. And he shall be like a tree planted by the river, bearing fruit in season, his leaf also not withering; and whatever he does will prosper.⁴⁸ This book of the law shall not depart out of your mouth; but you should meditate in it day and night, that you may observe to do according to all that is written therein; for then you will make your way prosperous and have good success.⁴⁹

Finally, I wish above all things that you may prosper and be in health, even as your soul prospers.⁵⁰

References:

1) Psalms 35:27 2) Joshua 1:7 3) Deuteronomy 29:9
4) I Kings 2:3 5) Joshua 1:7b
6) Deuteronomy 28:2–6, 8, 11–13 7) Proverbs 10:22
8) Proverbs 23:4 9) Proverbs 28:22 10) Proverbs 22:4
11) Proverbs 10:6 12) Proverbs 28:20 13) Proverbs 21:20
14) Proverbs 15:6 15) Proverbs 13:11 16) Proverbs 22:16
17) Proverbs 27:24 18) Proverbs 23:5 19) Proverbs 11:28
20) Proverbs 3:16 21) Proverbs 8:18 22) Proverbs 8:17
23) Proverbs 8:20 24) Proverbs 8:21 25) Proverbs 11:16
26) Proverbs 11:4 27) Proverbs 21:17 28) Proverbs 21:5
29) Proverbs 28:19 30) Proverbs 10:4 31) Proverbs 24:4
32) II Corinthians 8:9 33) Proverbs 13:22
34) Ecclesiastes 2:26 35) Deuteronomy 8:18
36) Psalms 112:1-3 37) Ecclesiastes 5:19 38) Isaiah 48:15
39) Psalms 3:8 40) Galatians 3:14 41) Hebrews 6:14
42) Deuteronomy 30:19 43) Proverbs 22:1
44) Psalms 62:10 45) I Samuel 2:7 46) Mark 10:23
47) I Corinthians 10:24 48) Psalms 1:1–3
49) Joshua 1:8 50) III John 1:2

SECTION II

*REAL ANSWERS
FOR
REAL LIFE SITUATIONS*

CHAPTER 46

Things To Remember When . . .
YOUR BOSS IS UNFAIR

He that does wrong shall receive for the wrong which he has done; and there is no respect of persons.[1] Nevertheless, do all things without murmurings and disputings,[2] not rendering evil for evil unto any man; but ever following that which is good, both among yourselves and to all men.[3] Love your enemies, bless them that curse you, do good to them that hate you, and pray for them which despitefully use you, and persecute you.[4]

Judge not and you shall not be judged;[5] for with what judgment you judge, you shall be judged; and with what measure you mete, it shall be measured to you again.[6] Condemn not and you shall not be condemned; forgive, and you shall be forgiven.[5]

When you stand praying, forgive, if you have ought against any; that your Father also which is in heaven may forgive you your trespasses.[7] But if you forgive not men their trespasses, neither will your Father forgive your trespasses.[8] Bear with each other and forgive each other, if any man have a quarrel against any; even as Christ forgave you, so must you forgive,[9] not just seven times, but until seventy times seven.[10] Don't give place to the devil![11]

These things I command you, that you love one another,[12] and whosoever shall compel you to go a mile, go with him two.[13] For I am persuaded, that neither death nor life, nor angels, nor principalities, nor powers, nor things present, nor things to come, nor height, nor depth, or any other creature, shall be able to separate us from the love of God, which is in Christ Jesus our Lord.[14]

Abstain from all appearance of evil,[15] and be kind one to another, tenderhearted, forgiving one another, even as God for Christ's sake has forgiven you,[16] bearing in mind that love is long suffering, and kind; love does not envy or boast, it is not puffed up, it does not behave itself unseemly, or seek its own way, love is not easily provoked, and thinks no evil; love bears all things, believes all things, hopes all things and endures all things. Love never fails.[17]

If you bring your gift before the altar, and there remember that your brother has ought against you; leave your gift before the altar, and go your way; first be reconciled to your brother, and then come and offer your gift.[18]

Pray without ceasing. In everything give thanks; for this is the will of God in Christ Jesus concerning you.[19] And we know that all things work together for good to them that love God, to them who are the called according to his purpose.[20]

References:

1) Colossians 3:25 2) Philippians 2:14
3) I Thessalonians 5:15 4) Matthew 5:44 5) Luke 6:37
6) Matthew 7:2 7) Mark 11:25 8) Matthew 6:15
9) Colossians 3:13 10) Matthew 18:22
11) Ephesians 4:27 12) John 15:17 13) Matthew 5:41
14) Romans 8: 38–39 15) I Thessalonians 5:22
16) Ephesians 4:32 17) I Corinthians 13: 4–5, 7–8
18) Matthew 5:23-24 19) I Thessalonians 5:17–18
20) Romans 8:28

CHAPTER 47

Things To Remember When . . .

EVERYTHING THAT CAN GO WRONG - DOES!

In the world, you will have tribulation, but be of good cheer for Jesus overcame the world,[1] so glory in tribulations, knowing that tribulation works patience, and patience, experience; and experience, hope; and hope won't disappoint you, because the love of God is shed abroad in your heart by the Holy Ghost which is given to you.[2]

In fact, you must through much tribulation enter into the kingdom of God;[3] knowing this, that the trying of your faith worketh patience. But let patience have her perfect work that you may be perfect and entire wanting nothing.[4]

In every situation, give thanks; for this is the will of God in Christ Jesus concerning you.[5] Rejoice evermore[6] in the Lord always; and again I say rejoice,[7] and keep rejoicing in hope; be patient in tribulation and continue praying always.[8] For our light affliction, which is but for a moment, worketh for us a far more exceeding and eternal weight of glory.[9] After all, neither death, nor life, nor angels, nor principalities, nor powers, nor things present, nor things to come, nor height, nor depth, or any other creature, shall be able to separate us from the love of God, which is in Christ Jesus our Lord.[10] And all things work together for good to them that love God, to them who are the called according to His purpose.[11] Remember that He comforts us in all our tribulation, that we may be able to comfort them which are in any trouble, by the comfort wherewith we ourselves are comforted of God.[12]

References:

1) John 16:33 2) Romans 5:3-5 3) Acts 14:22
4) James 1:3,4 5) I Thessalonians 5:18
6) I Thessalonians 5:16 7) Philippians 4:4
8) Romans 12:12 9) II Corinthians 4:17
10) Romans 8:38,39 11) Romans 8:28
12) II Corinthians 1:4

CHAPTER 48

Things To Remember When . . .
SOMEONE AT WORK RUBS YOU THE WRONG WAY - ALL THE TIME!

Love your enemies, bless them that curse you, do good to them which hate you, and pray for them which despitefully use you and persecute you; that you may be the children of your Father which is in heaven: for He makes the sun to rise on the evil and the good, and sends rain on the just and the unjust.[1]

Take heed to yourselves: if your brother trespass against you, rebuke him: and if he repents, forgive him.[2] For if you forgive men their trespasses, your heavenly Father will also forgive you. But if you don't forgive men their trespasses neither will your Father forgive your trespasses.[3] How often should you forgive a brother that sins against you? Till seven times? No! But until seventy times seven.[4] Yes, forbear one another, and forgive one another, if any man has a quarrel against any: even as Christ forgave you, so also you should do.[5]

Do not render evil for evil, or railing for railing,[6] letting evil overcome you, but overcome evil with good.[7] For the Lord has said, "Vengeance belongs to me. I will recompense," says the Lord.[8] For he that will love life, and see good days, let him refrain his tongue from evil, and his lips that they speak no guile,[9] letting all bitterness, wrath, anger, clamor and evil speaking, be put away from you with all malice.[10] Yes, be kindly affectioned one to another with brotherly love; in honor preferring one another,[11] considering how we may motivate each other to love and good works.[12] Love one another as Jesus loved you,[13] for love is of God; and everyone that loves is born of God, and knows God.[14]

You have need of patience, that after you have done the will of God, you will receive the promise;[15] knowing this, that the trying of your faith works patience. But let patience have her perfect work, that you may be perfect and entire, lacking nothing.[16] Wherefore, seeing we also are compassed about with so great a cloud of witnesses, let us lay aside every weight, and the sin which does so easily beset us, and let us run with patience the race that is set before us.[17]

Cease from anger, and forsake wrath,[18] for evil doers shall be cut off: but those who wait upon the Lord, shall inherit the earth.[19] Whatever you do, don't answer a fool according to his folly, lest you also be like him.[20] So he that is slow to wrath is of great understanding[21] and knows that a soft answer turns away wrath, but grievous words stir up anger.[22]

And remember, in your anger, do not sin, neither let the sun go down on your wrath nor give place to the devil.[23]

References:

1) Matthew 5:44,45 2) Luke 17:3 3) Matthew 6:14,15
4) Matthew 18:21,22 5) Colossians 3:13 6) I Peter 3:9
7) Romans 12:21 8) Hebrews 10:30 9) I Peter 3:10
10) Ephesians 4:31 11) Romans 12:10
12) Hebrews 10:24 13) John 13:34 14) I John 4:7
15) Hebrews 10:36 16) James 1:3,4 17) Hebrews 12:1
18) Psalms 37:8 19) Psalms 37:9 20) Proverbs 26:4
21) Proverbs 14:29 22) Proverbs 15:1
23) Ephesians 4:26,27

CHAPTER 49

Things To Remember When . . .
YOU EXPERIENCE A BIG DISAPPOINTMENT AT WORK

Rejoice greatly, though now for a season, if need be, you are in heaviness through many trials; that the trial of your faith, being much more precious than gold that perishes, though it be tried with fire, might be found unto praise and honor and glory at the appearing of Jesus Christ: whom having not seen, you love; in whom though now you see Him not, yet believing, you rejoice with joy unspeakable and full of glory; receiving the end of your faith, even the salvation of your souls.[1]

We are troubled on every side, yet not distressed; we are perplexed, but not in despair; persecuted, but not forsaken; cast down, but not destroyed.[2] So cast not away therefore your confidence which has great recompense of reward;[3] being confident of this very thing, that He which has begun a good work in you will perform it until the day of Jesus Christ.[4] Besides, you have need of patience, that after you have done the will of

God, you may receive the promise.[5]

Do not let you heart be troubled,[6] though you walk in the midst of trouble, God will revive you;[7] His rod and staff will comfort you.[8] A just man falls seven times, and rises up again;[9] he will not be utterly cast down for the Lord upholds him with His hand.[10] In fact, the Lord upholds all that fall and raises up all those that be bowed down.[11] So think it not strange concerning the fiery trial, as though some strange thing has happened to you: But rejoice, inasmuch as you are partakers of Christ's sufferings; that when His glory shall be revealed, you may be glad also with exceeding joy.[12] For many are the afflictions of the righteous; but the Lord delivers him out of them all.[13]

Be of good courage, and He will strengthen your heart, all you that hope in the Lord,[14] for He has said, I will never leave you, nor forsake you,[15] lo, I am with you always, even unto the end of the world.[16] And let us not be weary in well doing, for in due season we shall reap, if we faint not.[17]

Pray without ceasing, in everything give thanks; for this is the will of God in Christ Jesus concerning you.[18] And God is able to make all grace abound toward you; that you, always having all sufficiency, in all things, may abound to every good work,[19] for you can do all things through Christ who strengthens you.[20] The Lord increases His people greatly; making them stronger than their enemies,[21] and he that has clean hands shall be stronger and stronger.[22]

And remember, the eye of the Lord is upon them that fear Him,[23] and He takes pleasure in them that hope in His mercy.[24]

References:

1) I Peter 1:6-9 2) II Corinthians 4:8,9 3) Hebrews 10:35
4) Philippians 1:6 5) Hebrews 10:36 6) John 14:1
7) Psalms 138:7 8) Psalms 23:4 9) Proverbs 24:16
10) Psalms 37:24 11) Psalms 145:14 12) I Peter 4:12,13
13) Psalms 34:19 14) Psalms 31:24 15) Hebrews 13:5
16) Matthew 28:20 17) Galatians 6:9
18) I Thessalonians 5:17,18 19) II Corinthians 9:8
20) Philippians 4:13 21) Psalms 105:24 22) Job 17:9
23) Psalms 33:18 24) Psalms 147:11

CHAPTER 50

Things To Remember When . . .

YOU WANT TO SHARE THE LORD WITH A CO-WORKER

Don't be ashamed of the testimony of our Lord[1] or of the gospel of Christ; for it is the power of God unto salvation, to him that believes.[2] And whoever therefore will confess Jesus before men, Jesus will also confess him before the Father which is in heaven. But whoever denies Jesus before men, Jesus will deny him before the Father.[3]

He that wins souls is wise,[4] and he that converts the sinner from the error of his way will save a soul from death, and hide a multitude of sins.[5] Don't you realize that he that has the Son has life; and he that doesn't have the Son doesn't have life?[6] The Son of man came to save that which was lost.[7] For God loved the world so much, that He gave His only Son that whoever would believe in Him, would not perish, but have life everlasting. For God didn't send His Son into the world to condemn it, but that the world through Him might be saved.[8] So go into all the world and tell the good news to every creature;[9] and as many as receive Jesus, to them

He gives the power to become the sons of God, even to them that believe on His name.[10] And there will be more joy in heaven over one sinner that repents than over ninetynine just persons which need no repentance.[11]

Behold, He stands at the door and knocks; if any man hears His voice, and opens the door, He will come in to him, and will sup with him.[12] For He came not to call the righteous to repentance, but sinners.[13] Yet while we were sinners, Christ died for us which demonstrated God's great love for us.[14] Yes, all have sinned, and come short of the glory of God,[15] as by one man (Adam), sin entered into the world, and death by sin, and so death passed upon all men.[16] For the wages of sin is death; but the gift of God is eternal life through Jesus Christ our Lord.[17] For by grace are you saved through faith; and that not of yourselves; it is the gift of God, not of works, lest any man should boast.[18]

Brethren, if any man be overtaken in a fault, you which are spiritual, restore such a one in the spirit of meekness; considering yourself, lest you also be tempted.[19] Judge not that you be not judged,[20] speaking evil of no man,[21] for we all lived in times past, in the lusts of our flesh, fulfilling the desires of the flesh and of the mind, and were by nature the children of wrath, even as others.[22] But God has delivered us from the power of darkness, and has translated us into the kingdom of His dear Son;[23] to preach the gospel to the poor[24] and the meek,[25] to heal the brokenhearted,[24] to proclaim liberty to the captives[25] and recovering of sight to the blind[24] and the opening of the prison to them that are bound.[25]

These things were written to you that believe in the name of the Son of God; that you may know that you have eternal life.[26] For the word is near you, even in your mouth, and in your heart, that if you confess with your mouth the Lord Jesus, and believe in your heart that God has raised Him from the dead, you will be saved. For with the heart, man believes unto righteousness and with the mouth confession is made unto salvation.[27]

References:

1) II Timothy 1:8   2) Romans 1:16   3) Matthew 10:32, 33
4) Proverbs 11:30   5) James 5:20   6) I John 5:12
7) Matthew 18:11   8) John 3:16,17   9) Mark 16:15
10) John 1:12   11) Luke 15:7   12) Revelation 3:20
13) Luke 5:32   14) Romans 5:8   15) Romans 3:23
16) Romans 5:12   17) Romans 6:23   18) Ephesians 2:8,9
19) Galatians 6:1   20) Matthew 7:1   21) Titus 3:2
22) Ephesians 2:3   23) Colossians 1:13   24) Luke 4:18
25) Isaiah 61:1   26) I John 5:13   27) Romans 10:8-10

CHAPTER 51

Things To Remember When . . .
YOU NEED
PATIENCE - NOW!

Know this, that the trying of your faith works patience, but let patience have her perfect work, that you may be perfect and entire, lacking nothing.[1] For you have need of patience, that, after you have done the will of God, you might receive the promise.[2] So don't be slothful, but followers of them who through faith and patience inherit the promises.[3] And follow after righteousness, godliness, faith, love, patience and meekness.[4]

Wait on the Lord, be of good courage,[5] waiting patiently for Him,[6] keeping His way,[7] and he shall strengthen your heart,[5] exalt you to inherit the land, give you meat in due season,[8] renew your strength, cause you to mount up with wings as eagles, to run and not be weary, to walk and not faint,[9] and to see the wicked when they are cut off.[7]

Glory also in your tribulations, knowing that tribulation works patience; and patience, experience; and experience, hope; and hope won't make you ashamed; because the love of God is shed abroad in your heart by the Holy Ghost which is given to you.[10] Understand that whatever things were written aforetime, were written for your learning, that you through patience and comfort of the scriptures might have hope.[11] Wherefore, seeing we also are compassed about with so great a cloud of witnesses, let us lay aside every weight, and the sin which does easily beset us, and let us run with patience the race that is set before us,[12] knowing that the patient in spirit is better than the proud in spirit.[13]

Be you also patient; establish your hearts; for the coming of the Lord draws near.[14] and after you have patiently endured, you will obtain the promise.[15] For the Lord is good unto them that wait for Him, to the soul that seeks Him.[16]

Put on therefore, as the elect of God, holy and beloved, bowels of mercies, kindness, humbleness of mind, meekness and long-suffering,[17] with all lowliness and meekness, with patience, forbearing one another in love.[18] Don't you know that the fruit of the Spirit is love, joy, peace, patience, kindness, goodness, faith, gentleness and self control?[19]

Therefore, turn to your God; keep mercy and judgment, and wait on your God continually.[20] He is the God of your salvation, and He will hear you.[21] Wait only on God, for your expectation is from Him.[22]

For the vision is yet for an appointed time, but at the end it shall speak, and not lie; though it tarry, wait for it; because it will surely come, it will not tarry.[23]

References:

1) James 1:3, 4 2) Hebrews 10:36 3) Hebrews 6:12
4) I Timothy 6:11 5) Psalms 27:14 6) Psalms 37:7
7) Psalms 37:34 8) Psalms 145:15 9) Isaiah 40:31
10) Romans 5:3-5 11) Romans 15:4 12) Hebrews 12:1
13) Ecclesiastes 7:8 14) James 5:8 15) Hebrews 6:15
16) Lamentations 3:25 17) Colossians 3:12
18) Ephesians 4:2 19) Galatians 5:22 20) Hosea 12:6
21) Micah 7:7 22) Psalms 62:5 23) Habakkuk 2:3

CHAPTER 52

Things To Remember When . . .
YOU'RE NOT SURE WHAT TO SAY

Even a fool, when he holds his peace, is counted wise: and he that shuts his lips is esteemed a man of understanding.[1] However, a fool will usually utter all his mind; but a wise man keeps it in till afterwards.[2]

Let your light so shine before men,[3] having your conversation honest among the Gentiles, whereas they speak against you as evil doers, that they may by your good works, which they shall behold, glorify God in the day of visitation.[4]

But the Comforter, which is the Holy Ghost, who the Father will send in My name, He shall teach you all things, and bring all things to your remembrance, whatsoever I have said to you.[5] And if they bring you to the synagogues and unto magistrates and powers, take no thought how or what thing you shall answer, or what you shall say, for the Holy Ghost shall teach you in the same hour what you ought to say.[6]

Bless them which persecute you; bless, and curse not,[7] and remember there is a time to keep silence and a time to speak.[8]

References:

1) Proverbs 17:28 2) Proverbs 29:11 3) Matthew 5:16
4) I Peter 2:12 5) John 14:26 6) Luke 12:11-12
7) Romans 12:14 8) Ecclesiastes 3:7

CHAPTER 53

What To Do When You Feel . . .
BURNED OUT
ON YOUR JOB

The Lord gives power to the faint; and to them that have no might, He increases strength. Even the youths shall faint and be weary, and the young men shall utterly fall: but they that wait upon the Lord shall renew their strength; they shall mount up with wings as eagles; they shall run and not be weary; and they shall walk and not faint.[1]

Submit yourselves therefore to God,[2] casting all your care upon Him, for He cares for you,[3] and resist the devil, and he will flee from you.[2] Be confident of this very thing, that He which has begun a good work in you will perform it until the day of Jesus Christ.[4] For it is God which works in you both to will and to do of His good pleasure.[5] And look unto Jesus, the author and finisher of our faith; who for the joy that was set before Him endured the cross, despising the shame, and is set down at the right hand of the throne of God.[6] What shall we say then? If God be for us, who can be against us?[7]

The Lord is my shepherd; I shall not want. He makes me to lie down in green pastures: He leads me beside the still waters. He restores my soul; He leads me in the paths of righteousness for His name's sake. Yea, though I walk through the valley of the shadow of death, I will fear no evil: for thou art with me; thy rod and thy staff they comfort me. Thou preparest a table before me in the presence of mine enemies: thou anointest my head with oil: my cup runneth over. Surely goodness and mercy shall follow me all the days of my life: and I will dwell in the house of the Lord forever.[8]

The Lord increases His people greatly; making them stronger than their enemies,[9] and he that has clean hands shall be stronger and stronger.[10] For God satisfies your mouth with good things; so that your youth is renewed like the eagles;[11] and when you walk in the midst of trouble, He will revive you,[12] for the Lord is with him that is of a contrite and humble spirit, to revive the spirit of the humble, and to revive the heart of the contrite ones.[13] Again, wait on the Lord:[14] be of good courage, and He will strengthen your heart,[15] according to His word.[16]

Come unto the Lord, all you that labor and are heavy laden, and He will give you rest.

Take His yoke upon you, and learn of Him; for He is meek and lowly in heart: and you shall find rest unto your souls.[17] For there remains a rest for the people of God,[18] so give thanks to God, which gives us the victory through our Lord Jesus Christ,[19] always causing us to triumph in Christ.[20] For whatever is born of God, overcomes the world: and this is the victory that overcomes the world, even our faith.[21] Come boldy unto the throne of grace, that you may obtain mercy, and find grace to help in time of need,[22] not being slothful, but followers of them who through faith and patience inherit the promises.[23] Neither be weary in well doing; for in due season you shall reap if you don't faint.[24] Don't be afraid; for God is with you: be not dismayed; for He is your God: He will strengthen you; yes, He will help you and uphold you with the right hand of His righteousness.[25] So press toward the mark for the prize of the high calling of God in Christ Jesus,[26] making your calling and election sure.[27]

Remember that you can do all things through Christ which strengthens you,[28] because greater is He that is in you than he that is in the world.[29]

References:

1) Isaiah 40:29–31 2) James 4:7 3) I Peter 5:7
4) Philippians 1:6 5) Philippians 2:13 6) Hebrews 12:2
7) Romans 8:31 8) Psalms 23:1-6 9) Psalms 105:24
10) Job 17:9 11) Psalms 103:5 12) Psalms 138:7
13) Isaiah 57:15 14) Psalms 27:14 15) Psalms 31:24
16) Psalms 119:28 17) Matthew 11:28-29
18) Hebrews 4:9 19) I Corinthians 15:57
20) II Corinthians 2:14 21) I John 5:4 22) Hebrews 4:16
23) Hebrews 6:12 24) Galatians 6:9 25) Isaiah 41:10
26) Philippians 3:14 27) II Peter 1:10
28) Philippians 4:13 29) I John 4:4

CHAPTER 54

What To Do When You Feel . . .

SOMEONE HAS STEPPED ON YOU TO GET AHEAD

Love your enemies, bless them that curse you, do good to them that hate you, and pray for them which despitefully use you and persecute you.[1] And when you stand praying, forgive, if you have ought against any; that your Father also which is in heaven may forgive you your trespasses.[2] For if you forgive men their trespasses, your heavenly Father will also forgive you. But if you don't forgive men their trespasses, neither will your Father forgive your trespasses.[3] Judge not, and you will not be judged: condemn not, and you will not be condemned: forgive, and you will be forgiven.[4]

And why behold the speck in your brother's eye and ignore the stick that is in your own eye? Will you offer to remove the speck from your brother's eye, when you have a stick in your own eye? You hypocrite, first remove the stick from your eye, so you can see clearly to remove the speck from your brother's eye.[5]

Do all things without murmurings and disputings,[6] recompensing to no man evil for evil[7] or insult for insult,[8] but ever follow that which is good, both among yourselves, and to all men.[9] For he that will love life, and see good days, let him refrain his tongue from evil, and his lips that they speak no guile,[8] following Christ's example who, when He was reviled, reviled not again; when He suffered, He threatened not; but committed Himself to Him that judges righteously.[10]

Therefore, let all bitterness, wrath, anger, clamor, and evil speaking be put away from you, with all malice,[11] being kindly affectioned one to another with brotherly love; in honor preferring each other.[12] Instead of being overcome by evil, overcome evil with good,[13] considering how you can motivate one another to love and good works.[14] Grasp this fact, that love is longsuffering and kind, never envying or boastful, or proud. Love is not rude, self seeking, irritable or resentful. Love bears all things, believes all things, hopes all things and endures all things. Love never fails.[15] So be kind to each other, tenderhearted, forgiving one another, even as God for Christ's sake has forgiven you.[16]

No weapon formed against you shall prosper,[17] for greater is He that is in you than he that is in the world.[18] So rejoice evermore, pray without ceasing, in everything give thanks: for this is the will of God in Christ Jesus concerning you.[19] And we know that all things work together for good to them that love God, to them who are the called according to His purpose.[20] For I am persuaded that neither death nor life, nor angels, nor principalities, nor powers, nor things present, nor things to come, nor height, nor depth, nor any other creature, shall be able to separate us from the love of God, which is in Christ Jesus our Lord.[21]

Beloved, think it not strange concerning the fiery trial which is to try you, as though some strange thing has happened to you. But rejoice,[22] and know that the trying of your faith works patience; but let patience have her perfect work, that you may be perfect and entire, lacking nothing.[23] For the eyes of the Lord are over the righteous, and His ears are open to their prayers: but the face of the Lord is against them that do evil.[24]

In your anger, don't sin or let the sun go down upon your wrath,[25] neither give place to the devil.[26] But be subject one to another, and be clothed with humility: for God resists the proud, and gives grace to the humble.[27] Abstain from every appearance of evil,[28] cease from anger and forsake wrath,[29] for we know Him that said, "Vengeance belongs to me. I will recompense," says the Lord.[30] And anyone who does wrong will be paid back for the wrong he has done: and there is no respect of persons.[31] Don't be deceived; God is not mocked: for whatever a man sows, that shall he also reap.[32]

References:

1) Matthew 5:44 2) Mark 11:25 3) Matthew 6:14,15
4) Luke 6:37 5) Matthew 7:3-5 6) Philippians 2:14
7) Romans 12:17 8) I Peter 3:9,10
9) I Thessalonians 5:15 10) I Peter 2:23
11) Ephesians 4:31 12) Romans 12:10 13) Romans 12:21
14) Hebrews 10:24 15) I Corinthians 13:4,5,7,8,
16) Ephesians 4:32 17) Isaiah 54:17 18) I John 4:4
19) I Thessalonians 5:16-18 20) Romans 8:28
21) Romans 8:38,39 22) I Peter 4:12,13
23) James 1:3,4 24) I Peter 3:12 25) Ephesians 4:26
26) Ephesians 4:27 27) I Peter 5:5
28) I Thessalonians 5:22 29) Psalms 37:8
30) Hebrews 10:30 31) Colossians 3:25
32) Galatians 6:7

CHAPTER 55

What To Do When You Feel . . .
LIKE GIVING UP

God gives power to the faint; and to them that have no might He increases strength. Even the youths shall faint and be weary, and the young men shall utterly fall:but they that wait upon the Lord shall renew their strength; they shall mount up with wings as eagles; they shall run and not be weary; and they shall walk and never faint.[1] Let us therefore come boldly unto the throne of grace, that we may obtain mercy and find grace to help in time of need.[2]

Cast all your cares upon Him for He cares for you.[3] Come to Jesus all you that labor and are heavy laden, and He will give you rest. Take His yoke upon you, and learn of Him; for He is meek and lowly in heart: and you will find rest unto your soul.[4]

You are of God,[5] and whatsoever is born of God overcomes the world[6] because greater is He that is in you than he that is in the world:[5] and this is the victory that overcomes the world, even our faith.[6] So now, you can do all things through Christ which strengthens you[7] and gives you the victory,[8] always causing you to triumph in Him.[9]

Don't be afraid, for God is with you: don't be dismayed for He is your God: He will strengthen you, yes He will help you and uphold you with the right hand of His righteousness.[10] Just wait on the Lord: be of good courage, and He shall strengthen your heart: wait, I say on the Lord,[11] for there is a rest to the people of God.[12]

No weapon that is formed against you shall prosper; and every tongue that shall rise against you in judgement, you shall condemn for this is the heritage of the servants of the Lord, and your righteousness is of God.[13] and if God be for you, who can be against you?[14] For God increases His people greatly making them stronger than their enemies,[15] and he that hath clean hands shall be stronger and stronger.[16]

Be confident of this very thing, that He which began a good work in you will perform it until the day of Jesus Christ,[17] for it is God which worketh in you both to will and to do of His good pleasure.[18]

The battle is not yours, but God's;[19] so look unto Jesus, the author and finisher of your faith,[20] and say unto the mountain facing you, "Be thou removed and cast into the sea", not doubting in your heart, but believing that those things that you say shall come to pass, and you will have whatsoever you say. Therefore, whatever things you desire, when you pray, believe that you receive them, and you shall have them.[21]

If you have run with the footmen, and they have wearied thee, then how can you contend with horses?[22] Be strengthened according to God's word.[23] He will never leave you nor forsake you.[24] He is with you always, even unto the end of the world.[25]

Be not slothful, but followers of them who through faith and patience inherit the promises.[26] Say of the Lord, He is my refuge and my fortress: my God, in whom I will trust.[27] Press toward the mark for the prize of the high calling of God in Christ Jesus,[28] not being weary in well doing; for in due season you shall reap, if you don't faint and give up![29]

References:

1) *Isaiah 40:29-31 2) Hebrews 4:16 3) I Peter 5:7*
4) *Matthew 11:28,29 5) I John 4:4 6) I John 5:4*
7) *Philippians 4:13 8) I Corinthians 15:57*
9) *II Corinthians 2:14 10) Isaiah 41:10 11) Psalms 27:14*
12) *Hebrews 4:9 13) Isaiah 54:17 14) Romans 8:31*
15) *Psalms 105:24 16) Job 17:9 17) Philippians 1:6*
18) *Philippians 2:13 19) II Chronicles 20:15*
20) *Hebrews 12:2 21) Mark 11:23,24 22) Jeremiah 12:5*
23) *Psalms 119:28 24) Hebrews 13:5 25) Matthew 28:20*
26) *Hebrews 6:12 27) Psalms 91:2 28) Philippians 3:14*
29) *Galatians 6:9*

CHAPTER 56

What To Do When You Feel . . .
LIKE REALLY TELLING SOMEONE OFF!

Keep your tongue from evil, and your lips from speaking guile,[1] for there is not a word in your tongue, that the Lord doesn't know it already.[2] And so let every man be swift to hear, slow to speak, slow to wrath: for the wrath of man does not work the righteousness of God.[3] He that is slow to anger[4] or wrath is of great understanding,[5] better than the mighty,[4] and knows that a soft answer turns away wrath: grievous words only stir up anger.[6]

He that is soon angry, deals foolishly,[7] but he that keeps his mouth and controls his tongue, keeps his soul from troubles.[8] For death and life are in the power of the tongue: and they that love it shall eat the fruit thereof.[9] So, put away from you a perverse mouth, and corrupt talk put far away from you.[10] For you are snared and taken with the words of your mouth,[11] and a man of great wrath shall suffer punishment.[12]

For we know Him that has said, "Vengeance

belongs to Me, and I will recompense," saith the Lord.[13] So, let all bitterness, wrath, anger, clamor, and evil speaking be put away from you with malice: and be kind to one another, tenderhearted, forgiving one another, even as God for Christ's sake has forgiven you.[14] And if you forgive men their trespasses, your heavenly Father will also forgive you, but if you don't forgive men their trespasses, neither will your heavenly Father forgive your trespasses.[15] But remember this, that whoever is angry with his brother without a cause shall be in danger of the judgment: and whoever insults his brother shall be in danger of the council: but whoever calls his brother a fool, shall be in danger of hell fire.[16]

With the tongue we bless God, even the Father; and with it curse men, which are made after the similitude of God. Out of the same mouth proceeds blessing and cursing. These things should not be so.[17] So, cease from anger, forsake wrath,[18] take heed to your ways that you don't sin with your tongue, and keep your mouth with a bridle while the wicked are before you.[19]

Remember, he that will love life, and see good days, let him refrain his tongue from evil, and his lips that they speak no guile.[20]

References:

1) Psalms 34:13 2) Psalms 139:4 3) James 1:19-20
4) Proverbs 16:32 5) Proverbs 14:29 6) Proverbs 15:1
7) Proverbs 14:17 8) Proverbs 21:23 9) Proverbs 18:21
10) Proverbs 4:24 11) Proverbs 6:2 12) Proverbs 19:19
13) Hebrews 10:30 14) Ephesians 4:31-32
15) Matthew 6: 14-15 16) Matthew 5:22
17) James 3:9-10 18) Psalms 37:8 19) Psalms 39:1
20) I Peter 3:10

CHAPTER 57

What To Do When You Feel . . .
TOTALLY EXHAUSTED

He giveth power to the faint; and to them that have no might He increases strength. Even the youths shall faint and be weary, and the young men shall utterly fall: but they that wait upon the Lord shall renew their strength: they shall mount up with wings as eagles; they shall run, and not be weary; and they shall walk, and not faint.[1] Yes, wait on the Lord; be of good courage, and He will strengthen your heart: wait, I say on the Lord,[2] and He shall exalt you to inherit the land: when the wicked are cut off, you will see it,[3] and He shall save you.[4]

Come to Jesus, all you that labor and are heavy laden, and He will give you rest. Take His yoke upon you, and learn of Him, for He is meek and lowly in heart: and you shall find rest for your soul.[5] For there remains a rest to the people of God.[6] Though you walk in the midst of trouble, God will revive you[7] and satisfy your mouth with good things, so that your youth is renewed like the eagles.[8]

Rest in the Lord, and wait patiently for Him: fret not yourself because of him who prospers in his way, because of the man who brings wicked devices to pass.⁹ For God will restore to you the years that the locust has eaten, the cankerworm and the caterpillar, and the palmerworm.¹⁰ The Lord dwells in the high and holy place, and with him also that is of a contrite and humble spirit, to revive the spirit of the humble and the heart of the contrite ones.¹¹

If you have run with the footmen, and they have wearied you, then how can you contend with horses?¹² So be renewed in the spirit of your mind,¹³ and put on the new man which is renewed in knowledge, after the image of Him that created him;¹⁴ For which cause we faint not; but though our outward man perish, yet the inward man is renewed day by day.¹⁵

The Lord increases His people greatly; and makes them stronger than their enemies,¹⁶ and he that has clean hands shall be stronger and stronger.¹⁷ So let us not be weary in well doing; for in due season we shall reap, if we faint not.¹⁸

The Lord is my shepherd; I shall not want. He makes me to lie down in green pastures: He leads me beside the still waters. He restoreth my soul: He leadeth me in the paths of righteousness for His name's sake. Yea, though I walk through the valley of the shadow of death, I will fear no evil: for thou art with me: thy rod and thy staff they comfort me. Thou preparest a table before me in the presence of mine enemies: thou anointest my head with oil; my cup runneth over. Surely goodness and mercy shall follow me all the days of my life: and I will dwell in the house of the Lord forever.[19]

References:

*1) Isaiah 40:29-31 2) Psalms 27:14 3) Psalms 37:34
4) Proverbs 20:22 5) Matthew 11:28,29 6) Hebrews 4:9
7) Psalms 138:7 8) Psalms 103:5 9) Psalms 37:7
10) Joel 2:25 11) Isaiah 57:15 12) Jeremiah 12:5
13) Ephesians 4:23 14) Colossians 3:10
15) II Corinthians 4:16 16) Psalms 105:24 17) Job 17:9
18) Galatians 6:9 19) Psalms 23:1-6*

CHAPTER 58

What To Do When You Feel . . .
TOO DEPRESSED
TO WORK

Blessed are you that weep now; for you shall laugh,[1] for the Lord has appointed unto you the oil of joy for mourning, the garment of praise for the spirit of heaviness, that you might be called trees of righteousness, the planting of the Lord, that He might be glorified.[2]

Why is your soul cast down and disquieted within you? Hope thou in God,[3] remember Him[4] and praise Him who is the health of your countenance and is your God.[3] The Lord thinks upon you and is your help and deliverer.[5] God is our refuge, our strength[6] and our shield,[7] a very present help in trouble.[6] He heals the broken in heart and binds up their wounds.[8]

Remove sorrow from your heart,[9] and don't let it be troubled; neither let it be afraid.[10] You believe in God, believe also in Jesus;[11] Being confident of this very thing, that He which began a good work in you will perform it until the day of Jesus Christ.[12] For it is God which worketh in you both to will and to do of His good pleasure.[13]

Rejoice in the Lord always, and again I say rejoice.[14] In everything give thanks for this is the will of God in Christ Jesus concerning you.[15] Our light affliction, which is but for a moment, worketh for us a far more exceeding and eternal weight of glory.[16]

Beloved, think it not strange concerning the fiery trial which is to try you, as though some strange thing happened to you: but rejoice inasmuch as you are partakers of Christ's sufferings; that, when His glory shall be revealed, you may be glad also with exceeding joy.[17]

Firmly understand that neither death, nor life, nor angels, nor principalities, nor powers, nor things present, nor things to come, nor height, nor depth, nor any other creature, shall be able to separate us from the love of God, which is in Christ Jesus our Lord.[18] In fact, don't ever fear, for God is with you; don't be dismayed, for He is your God; He will strengthen you, yes, He will help you, and uphold you with the right hand of His righteousness.[19]

Return to the Lord, and come with singing unto Zion; and everlasting joy shall be upon your head; you will obtain gladness and joy; and sorrow and mourning shall flee away.[20]

Bless God, the Father of our Lord Jesus Christ, the Father of mercies, and the God of all comfort, who comforts us in all our tribulation, that we may be able to comfort them which are in any trouble by the comfort wherewith we ourselves are comforted of God.[21] Remember that weeping may endure for a night, but joy comes in the morning![22]

Wait on the Lord: be of good courage, and He shall strengthen your heart,[23] always looking unto Jesus, the author and finisher of our faith,[24] whose blessing makes rich, and he adds no sorrow with it.[25]

You are of God, and have overcome, because greater is He that is in you than he that is in the world,[26] which means you can do all things through Christ which strengthens you.[27]

Finally, brethren, whatsoever things are true, whatsoever things are honest, whatsoever things are just, whatsoever things are pure, whatsoever things are lovely, whatsoever things are of good report; if there be any virtue, if there be any praise, think on these things![28]

References:

1) Luke 6:21 2) Isaiah 61:3 3) Psalms 42:11
4) Psalms 42:6 5) Psalms 40:17 6) Psalms 46:1
7) Psalms 33:20 8) Psalms 147:3 9) Ecclesiastes 11:10
10) John 14:27 11) John 14:1 12) Philippians 1:6
13) Philippians 2:13 14) Philippians 4:4
15) I Thessalonians 5:18 16) II Corinthians 4:17
17) I Peter 4:12,13 18) Romans 8:38,39 19) Isaiah 41:10
20) Isaiah 51:11 21) II Corinthians 1:3,4
22) Psalms 30:5 23) Psalms 27:14 24) Hebrews 12:2
25) Proverbs 10:22 26) I John 4:4 27) Philippians 4:13
28) Philippians 4:8

CHAPTER 59

What You Should Know When . . .
FACED WITH A DIFFICULT DECISION

The Lord will teach and instruct you in the way you should go, guiding you with His eye.[1] Be wise and listen to His counsel,[2] for it will guide you[3] and stand forever.[4]

Make His testimonies your delight, and they will counsel you.[5] Yes, God's word is a lamp unto your feet and a light unto your path.[6] Apply your heart unto instruction and your ears to the words of knowledge.[7] Keep your father's commandment and forsake not the law of your mother; bind them continually upon your heart and tie them about your neck. When you go, it shall lead you; when you sleep it shall keep you. For the commandment is a lamp, and the law is light, and reproofs of instruction are the way of life.[8]

The Lord will show you the path of life;[9] simply commit your works unto the Lord and your thoughts will be established.[10] Though your heart devises a plan, the Lord will direct your steps.[11]

The Spirit of truth will guide you into all truth,[12] and your ears will hear a word behind you saying, "This is the way, walk ye in it" when you turn to the right hand or to the left.[13] Place your trust in God as your rock and fortress, and for His name's sake, He will lead you and guide you.[14]

Without counsel, the people fall,[15] and purposes are disappointed,[16] but in the multitude of counsellors there is safety[15] and every purpose is established.[16] Only with good advice[17] and wise counsel should you make plans to war,[18] and don't seek the counsel of ungodly or wicked people.[19]

Trust in the Lord with all your heart and lean not unto your own understanding. In all your ways acknowledge Him, and He shall direct your paths.[20] The Lord will teach you to profit, lead you by the way you should go,[21] and direct your work in truth.[22] For His thoughts are not your thoughts, neither are your ways His ways. As the heavens are higher than the earth, so are His ways higher than your ways and His thoughts than your thoughts.[23]

Bless the Lord who gives you counsel and instructs you at night with your heart.[24] Remember that a man's life is not his own; it is not for man to direct his steps.[25] So seek the Lord early, thirsting and longing for Him, and the Lord will help you, and you will not be confounded. Set your face like a flint, and you shall not be ashamed.[26] If you lack wisdom, ask of God, who gives to all men liberally and without finding fault, and it shall be given you; only ask in faith.[27]

You have the mind of Christ,[28] so be confident, for God has not given you the spirit of fear, but of power, and of love, and of a sound mind.[29] And remember, God is not the author of confusion, but of peace.[30]

References:

1) Psalms 32:8 2) Proverbs 12:15 3) Psalms 73:24
4) Psalms 33:11 5) Psalms 119:24 6) Psalms 119:105
7) Proverbs 23:12 8) Proverbs 6:20-23 9) Psalms 16:11
10) Proverbs 16:3 11) Proverbs 16:9 12) John 16:13
13) Isaiah 30:21 14) Psalms 31:3 15) Proverbs 11:14
16) Proverbs 15:22 17) Proverbs 20:18 18) Proverbs 24:6
19) Psalms 1:1 20) Proverbs 3:5-6 21) Isaiah 48:17
22) Isaiah 61:8 23) Isaiah 55:8-9 24) Psalms 16:7
25) Jeremiah 10:23 26) Isaiah 50:7
27) James 1:5-6 28) I Corinthians 2:16 29) II Timothy 1:7
30) I Corinthians 14:33

CHAPTER 60

What You Should Know When . . .
YOU WANT A PROMOTION

Promotion comes neither from the east, nor the west, nor from the south, but God is the judge. He putteth down one and exalteth another.[1]

Whosoever shall exalt himself shall be abased; and he that shall humble himself shall be exalted.[2] Humble yourself therefore under the mighty hand of God[3] in His sight,[4] that He may lift you up[3] and exalt you in due time.[4] For God resists the proud, but gives grace to the humble.[5]

Exalt and embrace wisdom and she will promote you and honor you,[6] offering length of days in her right hand and riches and honor in her left hand.[7]

The fear of the Lord will instruct you in wisdom; and humility goes before honor.[8] In fact, it is humility and the fear of the Lord that bring wealth and honor and life.[9] Honor is no more appropriate for a fool than snow in the summer and rain during harvest.[10]

Wait on the Lord, keep His way, and He shall exalt you to inherit the land, and you will see the wicked cut off.[11] Remember that every man shall receive his own reward according to his own labor.[12]

References:

1) Psalms 75:6,7   2) Matthew 23:12   3) I Peter 5:6
4) James 4:10   5) James 4:6   6) Proverbs 4:8
7) Proverbs 3:16   8) Proverbs 15:33   9) Proverbs 22:4
10) Proverbs 26:1   11) Psalms 37:34
12) I Corinthians 3:8

CHAPTER 61

What You Should Know When . . .

YOU'RE SUDDENLY OUT OF WORK

Lift up your eyes to the hills from where your help comes, the Lord, who made heaven and earth.[1] Be glad and rejoice in His mercy: for He has considered your trouble, and knows the anguish of your soul. He has not given you into the enemy's hands: He has set your feet in a large place.[2] God brings you out of the horrible pit and the miry clay to set your feet upon a rock, and establish your goings.[3]

Let not your heart be troubled: you believe in God, believe also in Jesus.[4] Though you walk in the midst of trouble, He will revive you and perfect that which concerns you.[5] For the Lord is good, a stronghold in the day of trouble; and He knows them that trust in Him,[6] and has promised to supply all your need according to His riches in glory by Christ Jesus.[7]

We are troubled on every side, yet not distressed; we are perplexed, but not in despair; persecuted, but not forsaken; cast down, but not destroyed.[8] Wherein you greatly rejoice, though now for a season, if need be, you are in heaviness, through many trials; that the trial of your faith, being much more precious than of gold that perishes, though it be tried with fire, might be found unto praise and honor and glory at the appearing of Jesus Christ.[9] So be anxious for nothing; but in everything by prayer and supplication with thanksgiving let your requests be made known unto God. And the peace of God, which passes all understanding, will keep your hearts and minds through Christ Jesus.[10]

For we have not a high priest which cannot be touched with the feeling of our weaknesses; but was in all points tempted like as we are, yet without sin. So let us therefore come boldly to the throne of grace, that we may obtain mercy, and find grace to help in time of need;[11] humbling yourself under the mighty hand of God, that He may exalt you in due time; casting all your care upon Him, for He cares for you.[12] He is the Father of mercies, and the God of all comfort; who comforts us in all our tribulation, that we may be able to comfort them which are in any trouble, by the comfort wherewith we ourselves are comforted of God.[13]

I have been young, and now am old; yet

have I not seen the righteous forsaken, nor his seed begging bread.[14] The young lions do lack and suffer hunger; but they that seek the Lord shall not want any good thing.[15] And this is the confidence that we have in Him, that if we ask anything according to His will, He hears us; and if we know that He hears us, whatever we ask, we know that we have the petitions that we desired of Him.[16] Therefore, whatever things you desire, when you pray, believe that you receive them, and you shall have them.[17] For whosoever shall say unto this mountain, 'be removed and cast into the sea' and does not doubt in his heart, but shall believe that those things which he says shall come to pass, he shall have whatever he says.[18]

Heaven and earth will pass away, but His words shall not pass away.[19] They are forever settled in heaven.[20] Therefore, attend to them, incline your ear to them; don't let them depart from view; keep them in the midst of your heart. For they are life to those that find them, and health to all their flesh.[21] In fact, there has not failed one word of all His good promises,[22] for He is faithful and will establish you.[23]

Remember it is God's wish that you prosper and be in health, even as your soul prospers,[24] and that all things work together for

good to them who are the called according
to His purpose.[25]

References:

1) Psalms 121:1,2   2) Psalms 31:7,8   3) Psalms 40:2
4) John 14:1   5) Psalms 138:7, 8   6) Nahum 1:7
7) Philippians 4:19   8) II Corinthians 4:8   9) I Peter 1:6,7
10) Philippians 4:6,7   11) Hebrews 4:15,16
12) I Peter 5:6,7   13) II Corinthians 1:3,4
14) Psalms 37:25   15) Psalms·34:10   16) I John 5:14,15
17) Mark 11:24   18) Mark 11:23   19) Matthew 24:35
20) Psalms 119:89   21) Proverbs 4:20-22   22) I Kings 8:56
23) II Thessalonians 3:3   24) III John 1:2
25) Romans 8:28

CHAPTER 62

What You Should Know When . . .
THE BOSS YELLS AT YOU

Show respect to all men and fear God. Servants, be subject to your masters with all respect; not only to the good and gentle, but also to the harsh. For it is commendable, if a man for conscience toward God endures grief, suffering unjustly. For what credit is there, if, when you are buffeted for your faults, you take it patiently? But if, when you do well, you suffer for it and take it patiently, this is acceptable with God. To this you were called: because Christ suffered for you, leaving us an example, that you should follow His steps: Who did no sin, neither was guile found in His mouth: Who, when He was reviled, reviled not again; when He suffered, He threatened not; but committed Himself to Him that judges righteously.[1]

Recompense to no man evil for evil,[2] or insult for insult,[3] but ever follow that which is good, both among yourselves and to all men.[4] For he that will love life, and see good days, let Him refrain His tongue from evil, and his lips that they speak no guile.[3] Do not let evil overcome you, rather overcome evil with good,[5] forgiving men their trespasses, and your heavenly Father will also forgive you.[6]

Remember that a soft answer turns away wrath, but grievous words only stir up anger.[7] Wherefore, brethren, let every man be swift to hear, slow to speak, slow to wrath: for the wrath of man does not work the righteousness of God.[8] In your anger, don't sin, and don't let the sun go down upon your wrath.[9] Yes, cease from anger, and forsake wrath,[10] for he that is slow to wrath is of great understanding.[11] And let all bitterness, wrath, anger, clamor, and evil speaking be put away from you, with all malice.[12]

Dearly beloved, avenge not yourselves, but rather give place unto wrath: for it is written, "Vengeance is Mine; I will repay," says the Lord.[13] Anyone who does wrong will be paid back for the wrong he has done: and there is no respect of persons.[14] Yes, all of you, be subject one to another, and be clothed with humility: for God resists the proud, and gives grace to the humble.[15]

He that loves life should turn away from evil and do good; let him seek peace and pursue it. For the eyes of the Lord are over the righteous, and His ears are open to their prayers: but the face of the Lord is against them that do evil.[16] And when you stand praying, forgive if you have ought against any, that your Father also which is in heaven may forgive you your trespasses.[17] Furthermore, love your enemies, bless them that curse you, do good to them that hate you, and pray for them which despitefully use you, and persecute you.[18]

Remember to do all things without murmurings and disputings.[19]

References:

1) I Peter 2:17-23 2) Romans 12:17 3) I Peter 3:9
4) I Thessalonians 5:15 5) Romans 12:21
6) Matthew 6:14 7) Proverbs 15:1 8) James 1:19,20
9) Ephesians 4:26 10) Psalms 37:8 11) Proverbs 14:29
12) Ephesians 4:31 13) Romans 12:19
14) Colossians 3:25 15) I Peter 5:5 16) I Peter 3:10-12
17) Mark 11:25 18) Matthew 5:44 19) Philippians 2:14

CHAPTER 63

What You Should Know When . . .

YOU ARE HARASSED AT WORK FOR YOUR BELIEFS

Blessed are you when men shall revile you and persecute you and shall say all manner of evil against you falsely for My sake. Rejoice and be exceeding glad; for great is your reward in heaven: for so persecuted they the prophets which were before you.[1] Love your enemies, bless them that curse you, do good to them that hate you, and pray for them which despitefully use you and persecute you.[2] If you are reproached for the name of Christ, you are blessed, for the Spirit of glory and of God rests on you.[3]

You will be hated of all men for My name's sake: but he that endures to the end shall be saved.[4] For whoever will save his life shall lose it; and whoever will lose his life for My sake will find it.[5] The servant is not greater than his lord. If they persecuted Jesus, they will also persecute you.[6] Therefore, take pleasure in weaknesses, in reproaches, in necessities, in persecutions, in distresses for Christ's sake: for when you are weak, then are you strong.[7] And take no thought how or what you will answer, or what you will say; for the Holy Ghost will teach you in the same hour what you ought to say.[8]

Let your light so shine before men that they may see your good works and glorify your Father which is in heaven.[9] Keep your lifestyle honest among the Gentiles, that whereas they speak against you as evildoers, they may by your good works, which they shall behold, glorify God in the day of visitation.[10]

No weapon that is formed against you will prosper; and every tongue that shall rise against you in judgment, you shall condemn.This is the heritage of the servants of the Lord, and their righteousness is of God.[11] So submit yourselves therefore to God. Resist the devil, and he will flee from you.[12] For we wrestle not against flesh and blood, but against principalities, against powers, against the rulers of the darkness of this world, against spiritual wickedness in high places.[13] For the weapons of our warfare are not carnal, but mighty through God to the pulling down of strongholds.[14]

References:

1) Matthew 5:11,12 2) Matthew 5:44 3) I Peter 4:14
4) Matthew 10:22 5) Matthew 16:25 6) John 15:20
7) II Corinthians 12:10 8) Luke 12:11,12
9) Matthew 5:16 10) I Peter 2:12
11) Isaiah 54:17 12) James 4:7
13) Ephesians 6:12 14) II Corinthians 10:4

CHAPTER 64

What You Should Know When . . .
YOU NEED CONFIDENCE

In the fear of the Lord is strong confidence.[1] Let us therefore come boldly unto the throne of grace, that we may obtain mercy, and find grace to help in time of need;[2] for the Lord shall be your confidence.[3]

You are of God, and greater is He that is in you than he that is in the world.[4] Cast not away therefore your confidence, which has great recompense of reward. For you have need of patience, that, after you have done the will of God, you will receive the promise.[5] Be confident of this very thing, that He which has begun a good work in you will perform it until the day of Jesus Christ.[6] Then we may boldly say, 'the Lord is my helper, and I will not fear what man shall do unto me.'[7] For by Thee I have run through a troop; and by my God I have leaped over a wall.[8]

And this is the confidence that we have in Him, that, if we ask anything according to His will, He hears us: and if we know that He hears us, whatever we ask, we know that we have the petitions that we desired of

Him.⁹ Beloved, if our heart condemn us not, then have we confidence toward God. For if our heart condemn us, God is greater than our heart and knoweth all things.¹⁰

It is better to trust in the Lord than to put confidence in man.¹¹ We are the circumcision, which worship God in the Spirit, and rejoice in Christ Jesus, and have no confidence in the flesh.¹² And this is the word of the Lord..."not by might, nor by power, but My Spirit", says the Lord of hosts.¹³

He that believes on Jesus, the works that Jesus did, shall he do also; and greater works than these shall he do because Jesus is with the Father.¹⁴ When you pass through the waters, God will be with you; and through the rivers, they will not overflow you: when you walk through the fire, you will not be burned; neither will the flame kindle upon you.¹⁵ Nay, in all these things we are more than conquerors through Him that loved us,¹⁶ and we can do all things through Christ who strengthens us;¹⁷ in whom we have boldness and access with confidence through faith in Him.¹⁸

References:

1) Proverbs 14:26   2) Hebrews 4:16   3) Proverbs 3:26
4) I John 4:4   5) Hebrews 10:35,36
6) Philippians 1:6   7) Hebrews 13:6
8) Psalms 18:29   9) I John 5:14,15
10) I John 3:20,21   11) Psalms 118:8
12) Philippians 3:3   13) Zechariah 4:6
14) John 14:12   15) Isaiah 43:2
16) Romans 8:37   17) Philippians 4:13
18) Ephesians 3:12

CHAPTER 65

What To Do When . . .

YOU'RE ASKED TO DO SOMETHING UNETHICAL

My son, if sinners entice you, consent not. If they say, come with us, let us lay wait for blood, let us lurk privily for the innocent without cause: let us swallow them up alive as the grave; and whole, as those that go down into the pit: we shall find all precious substance, we shall fill our houses with spoil: cast in your lot among us; let us all have one purse; my son, walk not in the way with them; refrain your foot from their path: for their feet run to evil, and make haste to shed blood. Surely in vain the net is spread in the sight of any bird. And they lay wait for their own blood; they lurk privily for their own lives. So are the ways of every one that is greedy of gain; which takes away the life of the owners thereof.[1]

Gather not your soul with sinners, nor your life with bloody men,[2] and do not envy them, neither desire to be with them,[3] but continue to reverence the Lord all the day long,[4] having no fellowship with the unfruitful works of darkness, but rather reprove them.[5]

Blessed is the man who won't follow the advice of the wicked, or hang around with sinners, mocking the things of God, but he delights in God's law and meditates in it day and night. And he will be like a tree planted by a river, bringing forth fruit in season, none of his leaves withering and whatever he does shall prosper.[6]

Submit yourself to God,[7] putting on His whole armor and stand against the devil's schemes,[8] resisting him and he will flee from you.[7] So be sober, be vigilant, because your adversary the devil, as a roaring lion, walks about, seeking whom he may devour.[9]

God will not cast away a perfect man, neither will He help the evildoers,[10] so see to it that none of you suffer as a murderer, or as a thief, or as an evildoer, or as a busybody in other men's matters.[11]

Love not the world, neither the things that are in the world. If any man love the world, the love of the Father is not in him. For all that is in the world, the lust of the flesh, and the lust of the eyes, and the pride of life, is not of the Father, but is of the world. And the world passes away, and the lust thereof: but he that does the will of God abides forever.[12]

References:

1) Proverbs 1:10–19 2) Psalms 26:9
3) Proverbs 24:1 4) Proverbs 23:17
5) Ephesians 5:11 6) Psalms 1:3 7) James 4:7
8) Ephesians 6:11 9) I Peter 5:8
10) Job 8:20 11) I Peter 4:15 12) I John 2:15–17

CHAPTER 66

What To Do When . . .

YOU'RE FACED WITH A CRISIS

As for me, I will call upon God; and the Lord shall save me,[1] for the Lord is near unto them that call upon Him, to all that call upon Him in truth.[2] Yes, call upon the Lord in your day of trouble,[3] and He will hear you,[4] answer you and[3] deliver you[5] from all your fears,[6] honor you[5] and save you from all your troubles.[4] As for God, His way is perfect, the word of the Lord is tried and true; He is a buckler to all those that trust in Him.[7] For though you walk in the midst of trouble, He will revive you; He shall stretch forth His hand against the wrath of your enemies, and His right hand shall save you.[8]

Don't let your heart be troubled;[9] when you pass through the waters, God will be with you; and through the rivers, they shall not overflow you; when you walk through the fire, you will not be burned, neither shall the flame kindle upon you.[10]

For we have not a high priest which cannot

be touched with the feeling of our infirmities; but was in all points tempted like as we are, yet without sin. Let us therefore come boldly unto the throne of grace, that we may obtain mercy, and find grace to help in time of need.[11] For who shall separate us from the love of Christ? Shall tribulation, or distress, or persecution, or famine, or nakedness, or peril, or sword? For I am persuaded, that neither death, nor life, nor angels, nor principalities, nor powers, nor things present, nor things to come, nor height, nor depth, nor any other creature, shall be able to separate us from the love of God, which is in Christ Jesus our Lord.[12]

Put on the whole armor of God, that you may be able to stand against the wiles of the devil.[13] Yes, submit yourself to God. Resist the devil and he shall flee from you,[14] and having done all, stand.[15] For the weapons of our warfare are not carnal, but mighty through God to the pulling down of strongholds.[16] Therefore, no weapon formed against you shall prosper; and every tongue that rises up against you in judgment, you shall condemn. This is the heritage of the servants of the Lord, and their righteousness is of God.[17] Besides, we wrestle not against flesh and blood, but against principalities, against powers, against the rulers of the darkness of this world and against spiritual wickedness in high places.[18]

The Lord is your hiding place; He will preserve you from trouble; He will compass you about with songs of deliverance,[19] and the angel of the Lord will encamp round about them that fear Him, and deliver them.[20] So cast all your care upon Him, for He cares for you,[21] and is the source of your help.[22]

References:

1) Psalms 55:16   2) Psalms 145:18   3) Psalms 86:7
4) Psalms 34:6   5) Psalms 91:15   6) Psalms 34:4
7) Psalms 18:30   8) Psalms 138:7   9) John 14:1
10) Isaiah 43:2   11) Hebrews 4:15,16
12) Romans 8:35-39   13) Ephesians 6:11
14) James 4:7   15) Ephesians 6:13
16) II Corinthians 10:4   17) Isaiah 54:17
18) Ephesians 6:12   19) Psalms 32:7
20) Psalms 34:7   21) I Peter 5:7   22) Psalms 121:2

CHAPTER 67

What To Do When . . .
YOU'RE LIED ABOUT

When the proud forge a lie against you; determine to keep God's precepts with your whole heart.[1] Blessed is the man that makes the Lord his trust, and respects not the proud, nor such as turn aside to lies.[2]

The wicked are estranged from the womb: they go astray as soon as they are born, speaking lies.[3] In fact, they delight in lies: they bless with their mouth, but they curse inwardly,[4] but the mouth of them that speak lies shall be stopped.[5] Do not allow him that works deceit to dwell in your house; and him that tells lies to tarry in your sight.[6] A false witness shall not be unpunished, and he that speaks lies will perish[7] and not escape.[8] A man that bears false witness against his neighbor is a maul, and a sword, and a sharp arrow,[9] uttering lies[10] and deceit,[11] and he will perish.[12] Seven things are an abomination to the Lord; a proud look, a lying tongue, hands that shed innocent blood, a heart that plans wicked imaginations, feet that are swift in running to mischief, a false witness that speaks lies, and he that sows discord among the brethren.[13] The Lord abhors the bloody and deceitful man,[14] for He commanded that you should not steal, neither deal falsely, neither lie one to another.[15]

When the people flattered God with their mouth, and lied unto Him with their tongues; when their heart was not right with him, neither were they steadfast in their covenant; He being full of compassion, forgave their iniquity, and destroyed them not: yes, many a time He turned His anger away, and did not stir up all His wrath. For He remembered that they were but flesh; a wind that passes away, and comes not again.[16]

So blessed are you, when men shall revile you, and persecute you, and say all manner of evil against you falsely for My name's sake. Rejoice and be exceeding glad: for great is your reward in heaven.[17] But, love your enemies, bless them that curse you, do good to them that hate you, and pray for them which despitefully use you, and persecute you.[18]

Remember, recompense to no man evil for evil, and provide things honest in the sight of all men.[19]

References:

1) Psalms 119:69 2) Psalms 40:4
3) Psalms 58:3 4) Psalms 62:4
5) Psalms 63:11 6) Psalms 101:7
7) Proverbs 19:9 8) Proverbs 19:5
9) Proverbs 25:18 10) Proverbs 14:5
11) Proverbs 12:17 12) Proverbs 21:28
13) Proverbs 6:16-19 14) Psalms 5:6
15) Leviticus 19:11 16) Psalms 78:36-39
17) Matthew 5:11-12 18) Matthew 5:44
19) Romans 12:17

CHAPTER 68

What To Do When . . .
YOU REALIZE YOU HAVE COMPROMISED YOUR INTEGRITY

Be zealous therefore and repent,[1] confessing your faults one to another and praying for one another that you may be healed.[2] For if we confess our sins, He is faithful and just to forgive us our sins and to cleanse us from all unrighteousness.[3]

Accept the fact that you're not perfect yet, and do this one thing, forgetting those things which are behind, reaching forth unto those things which are ahead, press toward the mark for the prize of the high calling of God in Christ Jesus.[4] The apostle Paul said, "I do not understand my own actions; for what I would, that do I not; but what I hate, that do I. If then I do that which I would not, I consent unto the law that it is good. Now then it is no more I that do it, but sin that dwells in me. For I know that in me (that is, in my flesh), dwells no good thing: for to will is present with me; but how to perform that which is good I find not. For the good that I would, I do not: but the evil

which I would not, that I do. Now if I do
what I don't want to do, it is no more I that
do it, but sin that dwells in me. I find then a
law, that, when I would do good, evil is present with me. For I delight in the law of God
after the inward man: but I see another law
in my members, warring against the law of
my mind, and bringing me into captivity to
the law of sin which is in my members. O
wretched man that I am! Who shall deliver
me from the body of this death? I thank God
through Jesus Christ our Lord. So then with
the mind I myself serve the law of God; but
with the flesh, the law of sin. There is
therefore now no condemnation to them
which are in Christ Jesus, who walk not after
the flesh, but after the Spirit. For the law of
the Spirit of life in Christ Jesus hath made
me free from the law of sin and death."[5]

The Lord is good, and ready to forgive; and
plenteous in mercy unto all them that call
upon Him,[6] in whom we have redemption
through His blood, even the forgiveness of
sins,[7] that He may be feared.[8]

Therefore, if you bring your gift to the altar
and there remember that your brother has
ought against you, leave your gift at the altar,
and go your way; first be reconciled to your
brother, and then come and offer your gift.[9]
And if you forgive men their trespasses, your

heavenly Father will also forgive you[10] and restore unto you the joy of your salvation.[11]

References:

1) Revelation 3:19 2) James 5:16
3) I John 1:9 4) Philippians 3:13,14
5) Romans 7:15-8:2 6) Psalms 86:5
7) Ephesians 1:7 8) Psalms 130:4
9) Matthew 5:23,24 10) Matthew 6:14
11) Psalms 51:12

CHAPTER 69

What To Do When . . .
YOU HAVE WRONGED
A FELLOW WORKER

If you bring your gift to the altar and there remember that your brother has ought against you, leave your gift before the altar, and go first be reconciled to your brother, and then come and offer your gift.[1] If we say that we have no sin and have never sinned, we deceive ourselves; we make Him a liar[2] and the truth and the word are not in us.[3]

As many as God loves, He rebukes and chastens: be zealous therefore, repent,[4] and confess your sins for He is faithful and just to forgive us our sins, and to cleanse us from all unrighteousness.[5]

In many things we offend all. If any man offend not in word, the same is a perfect man, and able also to bridle the whole body.[6] But if we sin, we have an advocate with the Father, Jesus Christ the righteous.[7]

Agree with your adversary quickly, before you get to court, lest you be delivered to the judge, and the judge delivers you to the officer and you be cast into prison.[8]

Realize that you are not perfect yet, but do this one thing, forget those things which are behind, and reach forward to those things which are ahead, and press toward the mark for the prize of the high calling of God,[9] knowing that all things work together for good to them that love God, to them who are the called according to His purpose.[10]

References:

1) Matthew 5:23,24   2) I John 1:10   3) I John 1:8
4) Revelation 3:19   5) I John 1:9   6) James 3:2
7) I John 2:1   8) Matthew 5:25   9) Philippians 3:13,14
10) Romans 8:28

CHAPTER 70

What To Do When . . .

YOUR CO-WORKERS ARE IN TOTAL DARKNESS

Let your light so shine among men, that they may see your good works, and glorify your Father which is in heaven,[1] and be blameless and harmless, the sons of God.[2] For God who commanded the light to shine out of darkness, has shined in our hearts, to give the light of the knowledge of the glory of God in the face of Jesus Christ.[3]

Jesus is the light of the world; he that follows Him shall not walk in darkness, but shall have the light of life.[4] So walk in the light while you have it, lest darkness come upon you, yes, believe in the light that you may be the children of light.[5]

No man when he lights a candle, hides it secretly or puts it under a bushel, but on a candlestick that they which come in may see the light.[6] And have no fellowship with the unfruitful works of darkness, but rather reprove them, for it is a shame even to speak of those things which are done by them in secret.[7] Do this so their eyes may be opened, and to turn them from darkness to light, and from the power of Satan unto God, that they may receive forgiveness of sins, and inheritance among them which are sanctified;[8] knowing that all things that are reproved are made manifest by the light, for it is light that makes all things visible.[9]

You are children of light, and children of the day, not of the night or darkness,[10] so cast off the works of darkness, and put on the armor of light,[11] not sleeping like others, but watching and remaining sober.[12]

Jesus came not to call the righteous, but sinners to repentance,[13] so preach the word; be instant in season and out of season;[14] receive the power of the Holy Ghost to be witnesses,[15] rebuke, reprove, exhort with all longsuffering and doctrine,[14] sanctifying the Lord in your heart, and be ready always to give an answer to every man that asks you a reason of the hope that is in you with meekness and fear.[16]

Tell them that God so loved the world, that He gave His only begotten Son, that whosoever would believe in Him should not perish, but have everlasting life. For God sent not His Son into the world to condemn the world; but that the world through him might be saved;[17] that if they would confess

with their mouth the Lord Jesus, and believe
in their heart that God has raised Him from
the dead, they will be saved. For with the
heart man believes unto righteousness, and
with the mouth confession is made unto
salvation.[18]

For you see, the Son of man came to seek
and to save that which was lost,[19] demon-
strating His love for us, in that, while we
were yet sinners, Christ died for us.[20] He is
not slack concerning His promise, as some
men count slackness; but is longsuffering
towards us, not willing that any should
perish, but that all should come to repentance.[21]

Remember, where sin abounds, God's grace
does much more abound.[22]

References:

1) Matthew 5:16 2) Philippians 2:15 3) II Corinthians 4:6
4) John 8:12 5) John 12:35,36 6) Luke 11:33
7) Ephesians 5:11,12 8) Acts 26:18 9) Ephesians 5:13
10) I Thessalonians 5:5 11) Romans 13:12
12) I Thessalonians 5:6 13) Luke 5:32 14) II Timothy 4:2
15) Acts 1:8 16) I Peter 3:15 17) John 3:16,17
18) Romans 10:9,10 19) Luke 19:10 20) Romans 5:8
21) II Peter 3:9 22) Romans 5:20

CHAPTER 71

What To Do When . . .
THERE IS MORE TO DO THAN TIME ALLOWS

Walk in wisdom, making the very most of time seizing every opportunity.[1]

Biblical Occurrences of Delegation:

1. Moreover thou shalt provide out of all the people able men, such as fear God, men of truth, hating covetousness; and place such over them to be rulers of thousands, and rulers of hundreds, rulers of fifties, and rulers of tens: and let them judge the people at all seasons: and it shall be, that every great matter they shall bring unto thee, but every small matter they shall judge: so shall it be easier for thyself, and they shall bear the burden with thee. If thou shalt do this thing, and God command thee so, then thou shalt be able to endure, and all this people shall also go to their place in peace. So Moses harkened to the voice of his father-in-law, and did all that he had said. And Moses chose able men out of all Israel, and made them heads over the people, rulers of thousands, rulers of hundreds, rulers of fif-

ties, and rulers of tens. And they judged the people at all seasons; the hard cases they brought unto Moses, but every small matter they judged themselves.[2]

2. Let Pharaoh do this, and let him appoint officers over the land, and take up the fifth part of the land of Egypt in the seven plenteous years.[3]

3. And he will appoint him captains over thousands, and captains over fifties; and will set them to ear his ground, and to reap his harvest, and to make his instruments of war, and instruments of his chariots.[4]

4. And I said unto them, Let not the gates of Jerusalem be opened until the sun be hot; and while they stand by, let them shut the doors, and bar them: and appoint watches of the inhabitants of Jerusalem, every one in his watch, and every one to be over against his house.[5]

5. And let the king appoint officers in all the provinces of his kingdom, that they may gather together all the fair young virgins unto Shushan the palace, to the house of the women unto the custody of Hege the king's chamberlain, the keeper of the women; and let their things for purification be given them.[6]

6. Wherefore brethren, look ye out among you seven men of honest report, full of the Holy Ghost and wisdom, whom we may appoint over this business.[7]

7. For I am a man under authority, having soldiers under me: and I say to this man, Go, and he goeth; and to another, Come, and he cometh; and to my servant, Do this, and he doeth it.[8]

References:

1) Colossians 4:5 2) Exodus 18:21-26
3) Genesis 41:34 4) I Samuel 8:12 5) Nehemiah 7:3
6) Esther 2:3 7) Acts 6:3 8) Matthew 8:9

CHAPTER 72

What To Do When . . .

YOU'RE TOO SICK TO WORK

Is any sick among you? Let him call for the elders of the church; and let them pray over him, anointing him with oil in the name of the Lord; and the prayer of faith shall save the sick, and the Lord shall raise him up; and if he has committed sins, they shall be forgiven him; yes, confess your faults one to another, and pray for one another, that you may be healed, and the effectual fervent prayer of a righteous man is very powerful.[1]

Serve the Lord your God, and He will bless your bread and water, and take sickness away from your midst.[2] In fact the Lord will take away from you all sickness and will put none of the evil diseases of Egypt upon you,[3] for He is the Lord which heals you.[4]

Cast your burden upon the Lord, and He will sustain you,[5] for Jesus Himself bare our sins in His own body on the tree, that we being dead to sins, should live unto righteousness: by whose stripes you were healed![6] And when you take communion, examine yourself and then eat of the bread and drink of the cup, for he that eats and drinks in an unworthy manner, eats and drinks damnation to himself, not discerning the Lord's body. It is for this reason that many are weak and sickly, and some have even died prematurely. For if we would judge ourselves, we would not be judged.[7]

Blessed be God, even the Father of our Lord Jesus Christ, the Father of mercies, and the God of all comfort; who comforts us in all our tribulation, that we may be able to comfort them which are in any trouble with the comfort that we were comforted with.[8]

Remember, these signs will follow those who believe; they shall use the authority of Jesus' name to cast out demons, speak in new tongues, even handle serpents without harm, and if they should drink any deadly thing, it will not hurt them; they shall lay hands upon the sick, and they shall recover.[9] Wherefore, comfort one another with these words.[10]

References:

1) *James 5:14-16* 2) *Exodus 23:25* 3) *Deuteronomy 7:15*
4) *Exodus 15:26* 5) *Psalms 55:22* 6) *I Peter 2:24*
7) *I Corinthians 11:28-31* 8) *II Corinthians 1:3,4*
9.*Mark 16:17,18* 10) *I Thessalonians 4:18*

CHAPTER 73

What To Do When . . .
SOMEONE YOU WORK WITH IS DISCOURAGED

God comforts you in your tribulation, that you may be able to comfort them which are in any trouble, with the same comfort that God comforted you with.[1] For God comforts those that are cast down[2] and wants you to comfort yourselves together, and edify each other[3] following after the things which make for peace.[4]

Be kindly affectioned one to another with brotherly love; in honor preferring one another[5] with all lowliness and meekness, with longsuffering, forbearing one another in love,[6] being kind to each other, tenderhearted, and forgiving one another, even as God for Christ's sake has forgiven you.[7] Let the word of Christ dwell in you richly in all wisdom; teaching and admonishing one another in psalms and hymns and spiritual songs, singing with grace in your heart to the Lord.[8]

Submit yourselves one to another in the fear of God,[9] considering each other to provoke unto love and to good works, not forsaking the assembling of yourselves together, as the manner of some is; but exhorting one another, and so much the more as you see the day approaching.[10]

Warn them that are unruly, comfort the feebleminded, support the weak, be patient toward all men,[11] and exhort one another daily, while it is called Today; lest any of you be hardened by the deceitfulness of sin.[12]

Love one another, as Christ loves you,[13] building up yourselves on your most holy faith, praying in the Holy Ghost[14] and being committed to the word of His grace, which is able also to build you up.[15] I am persuaded, brethren, that you also are full of goodness, filled with all knowledge, able also to admonish one another,[16] but God wants no schism in the body; but that the members of the body should have the same care one for another.[17] For brethren, you have been called unto liberty; only use not liberty for an occasion to the flesh, but by love, serve one another.[18]

Let us not judge one another,[19] but love one another[20] with a pure heart fervently,[21] being subject one to another, being clothed with humility: for God resists the proud, but gives grace to the humble.[22] And let nothing be done through strife or conceit; but in lowliness of mind let each esteem the other as better than themselves.[23]

Finally, be ye all of one mind, having compassion one of another, love as brethren, be pitiful, be courteous,[24] using hospitality one to another without grudging.[25] And confess your faults one to another, and pray for one another, that you may be healed, remembering also that the fervent prayer of a righteous man is powerful and effective.[26]

References:

1) II Corinthians 1:4 2) II Corinthians 7:6
3) I Thessalonians 5:11 4) Romans 14:19
5) Romans 12:10 6) Ephesians 4:2
7) Ephesians 4:32 8) Colossians 3:16 9) Ephesians 5:21
10) Hebrews 10:24,25 11) I Thessalonians 5:14
12) Hebrews 3:13 13) John 13:34 14) Jude 1:20
15) Acts 20:32 16) Romans 15:14
17) I Corinthians 12:25 18) Galatians 5:13
19) Romans 14:13 20) John 15:17 21) I Peter 1:22
22) I Peter 5:5 23) Philippians 2:3 24) I Peter 3:8
25) I Peter 4:9 26) James 5:16

CHAPTER 74

What The Bible Says About . . .
SEXUAL TEMPTATION AT WORK

There has no temptation taken you but such as is common to man: but God is faithful, who will not allow you to be tempted above that which you are able; but will with the temptation also make a way of escape, that you may be able to bear it.[1] Now the works of the flesh are manifest, which are these; adultery, fornication, uncleanness, lasciviousness, idolatry, witchcraft, hatred, variance, emulations, wrath, strife, seditions, heresies, envyings, murders, drunkenness, revellings, and such like, and they which do such things shall not inherit the kingdom of God.[2] In fact, because of these things, the wrath of God comes on the children of disobedience.[3] For this is the will of God, even your sanctification, that you should abstain from fornication: that every one should know how to possess his vessel in sanctification and honor; not in the lust of concupiscence, even as the Gentiles which know not God.[4]

Now the body is not for fornication, but for

the Lord; and the Lord for the body.⁵ So flee fornication, because every sin that a man commits is outside his body, but he that commits fornication, sins against his own body. Your body is the temple of the Holy Spirit, which is in you, as a gift from God. You are not your own, for you were bought with a price:therefore, glorify God in your body and in your spirit, which are God's.⁶ Nevertheless, to avoid fornication, let every man have his own wife and let every woman have her own husband,⁷ for fornication and all uncleanness and covetousness, should not be once named among you as is fitting among saints.⁸

Put on the Lord Jesus Christ, and make no provision for the flesh, to fulfill its lusts,⁹ for if you are Christ's then you have crucified the flesh with the affections and lusts.¹⁰ For all that is in the world, the lust of the flesh, and the lust of the eyes, and the pride of life, is not of the Father, but is of the world.¹¹ And don't you know that friendship with the world is enmity with God? Whosoever therefore will be a friend of the world is the enemy of God.¹² The world will pass away with the lusts thereof; but he that does the will of God abides forever.¹³

You have heard that it was said of them of old, do not commit adultery. But in reality, whoever looks on a woman to lust after her has committed adultery with her already in his heart.[14] This I say then, walk in the spirit, and you will not fulfill the lust of the flesh,[15] and brethren, whatsoever things are true, honest, just, pure, lovely or of good report; if there be any virtue, and if there be any praise,think on these things.[16] Watch and pray that you enter not into temptation; for the spirit is indeed willing, but the flesh is weak.[17] Blessed is the man that endures temptation, for when he is tried, he will receive the crown of life, which the Lord has promised to them that love Him. Let no man say when he is tempted, I am tempted of God: for God cannot be tempted of evil, neither does He tempt any man. But every man is tempted when he is drawn away of his own lust, and enticed. Then when lust has conceived, it brings forth sin: and sin, when it is finished, brings forth death.[18] So count it all joy when you fall into many temptations; knowing this, that the trying of your faith works patience. But let patience have her perfect work, that you may be perfect and entire, lacking nothing.[19]

The Lord knows how to deliver the godly out of temptations,[20] for we have not a high priest which cannot be touched with the feeling of our weaknesses; but was in all points tempted like as we are, yet without sin.[21] But if a man be overtaken with a fault, you which are spiritual, restore such a one in the spirit of meekness; considering yourself, lest you also be tempted.[22]

He that finds a wife, finds a good thing, and obtains favor of the Lord,[23] but let marriage be held in honor, and the bed undefiled for God will judge the immoral and the adulterers.[24] Don't you know that your bodies are the members of Christ? Should you then take the members of Christ and make them the members of a harlot? God forbid! He that is joined to a harlot is one body with her, for two, saith God, shall be one flesh.[25] But drink waters out of your own cistern, and running waters out of your own well. Let your fountain be blessed: and rejoice with the wife of your youth. Let her be as the loving hind and pleasant roe; let her breasts satisfy you at all times and always be ravished with her love. Why be ravished with a strange woman, and embrace the bosom of a stranger? For the ways of man are before the eyes of the Lord, and He ponders all his goings.[26]

King Solomon's Comments:

For the commandment is a lamp; and the law is light; and reproofs of instruction are the way of life: to keep thee from the evil woman, from the flattery of the tongue of a strange woman. Lust not after her beauty in thine heart; neither let her take thee with her eyelids. For by means of a whorish woman a man is brought to a piece of bread: and the adulteress will hunt for the precious life. Can a man take fire in his bosom, and his clothes not be burned? Can one go upon hot coals, and his feet not be burned? So he that goeth in to his neighbor's wife; whosoever toucheth her shall not be innocent.[27]

But whoso committeth adultery with a woman lacketh understanding: he that doeth it destroyeth his own soul. A wound and dishonor shall he get; and his reproach shall not be wiped away. For jealousy is the rage of a man: therefore he will not spare in the day of vengeance. He will not regard any ransom; neither will he rest content, though thou givest many gifts.[28]

Say unto wisdom, thou art my sister; and call understanding thy kinswoman: that they may keep thee from the strange woman, from the stranger which flattereth with her words. For at the window of my house I looked through my casement, and beheld among the simple ones, I discerned among the youths, a young man void of understanding, passing through the street near her corner; and he went the way to her house. In the twilight, in the evening, in the black and dark night: And, behold, there met him a woman with the attire of a harlot, and subtil of heart. She is loud and stubborn; her feet abide not in her house: Now is she without, now in the streets, and lieth in wait at every corner. So she caught him, and kissed him, and with an impudent face said unto him, 'I have peace offerings with me; this day have I payed my vows. Therefore came I forth to meet thee, diligently to seek thy face, and I have found thee. I have decked my bed with coverings of tapestry, with carved works, with fine linen of Egypt. I have perfumed by bed with myrrh, aloes, and cinnamon. Come, let us take our fill of love until the morning:let us solace ourselves with loves. For the goodman is not at home, he is gone on a long journey: he hath taken a bag of money with him, and will come home at the day appointed.' With her much fair speech she caused him to yield, with the flattering of her lips she forced him. He goeth after her straightway, as an ox goeth to the slaughter, or as a fool to the correction of the stocks; till a dart strike through his liver; as a bird hasteth to the snare, and knoweth not that it is for his life. Hearken unto me now therefore, O ye children, and attend to the words of my mouth. Let not thine heart decline to her ways, go not astray in her paths. For she hath cast down many wounded: yea, many strong men have been slain by her. Her house is the way to hell, going down to the chambers of death.[29]

References:

1) I Corinthians 10:13 2) Galatians 5:20-21
3) Colossians 3:5-6 4) I Thessalonians 4:3–5
5) I Corinthians 6:13 6) I Corinthians 6:18-20
7) I Corinthians 7:2 8) Ephesians 5:3
9) Romans 13:14 10) Galatians 5:24 11) I John 2:16
12) James 4:4 13) I John 2:17 14) Matthew 5:27-28
15) Galatians 5:16 16) Philippians 4:8
17) Matthew 26:41 18) James 1:12–15
19) James 1:2–4 20) II Peter 2:9 21) Hebrews 4:15
22) Galatians 6:1 23) Proverbs 18:22
24) Hebrews 13:4 25) I Corinthians 6:15-16
26) Proverbs 5:15-21 27) Proverbs 6:23-29
28) Proverbs 6:32-35 29) Proverbs 7:4-27

CHAPTER 75

What The Bible Says About . . .
GOSSIP

A gossip goes around revealing secrets.[1] The rumors they spread are like dainty morsels, going down into the innermost parts of the belly,[2] therefore, meddle not with him that flatters with his lips.[3] Where no wood is, the fire goes out, so where there is no gossip, the strife ceases.[4]

He that hides hatred with lying lips and he that utters slander is a fool.[5] And he that keeps his mouth, keeps his life; but he that opens wide his lips shall have destruction.[6] Therefore, keep your tongue from evil and your lips from speaking guile.[7] Don't you know that you are snared and taken with the words of your mouth?[8]

Speak no evil of any man, be gentle, showing all meekness unto all men,[9] for a wholesome tongue is a tree of life.[10] In fact, death and life are in the power of the tongue, and they that love it shall eat the fruit thereof.[11]

Do all things without murmurings and disputings,[12] letting all bitterness, and wrath, and anger, and clamor and evil speaking be put away from you, with all malice.[13] Yes, put off all these: anger, wrath, malice,and filthy communication.[14] Lying lips are an abomination to the Lord, but they that deal truly are his delight.[15]

Even so the tongue is a little member, and boasts great things. Behold, how great a matter a little fire kindleth![16] If any man offend not in word, the same is a perfect man, and able also to bridle the whole body.[17] In the multitude of words there wanteth no sin: but he that refraineth his lips is wise.[18]

For he that will love life and see good days, let him refrain his tongue from evil, and his lips that they speak no guile.[19] Yes, don't speak evil of one another. He that speaks evil of his brother and judges his brother, speaks evil of the law and judges the law. But if you judge the law, you are not a doer of the law, but a judge.[20]

Simply let your communication be yea, yea; nay, nay; for whatsoever is more than these cometh of evil.[21]

References:

1) Proverbs 11:13 2) Proverbs 26:22
3) Proverbs 20:19 4) Proverbs 26:20
5) Proverbs 10:18 6) Proverbs 13:3
7) Psalms 34:13 8) Proverbs 6:2
9) Titus 3:2 10) Proverbs 15:4
11) Proverbs 18:21 12) Philippians 2:14
13) Ephesians 4:31 14) Colossians 3:8
15) Proverbs 12:22 16) James 3:5
17) James 3:2 18) Proverbs 10:19
19) I Peter 3:10 20) James 4:11
21) Matthew 5:37

CHAPTER 76

What The Bible Says About . . .
HELPING SOMEONE IN NEED

If a brother or sister be naked, and destitute of daily food and you say to them, "Go in peace, be warm and eat hearty", and then don't give them food or clothes, what good does that do? It's not good enough to just have faith, because faith without action is dead.[1] Whoever gives even a cup of water in the name of Jesus, because he belongs to Christ, truly, he shall not lose his reward.[2] Therefore, to him that knows to do good, and does it not, to him it is sin.[3]

Then shall the King say unto them on His right hand, "Come ye blessed of My Father, inherit the kingdom prepared for you from the foundation of the world: for I was hungry, and you gave me meat; I was thirsty, and you gave me drink; I was a stranger, and you took me in: naked, and you clothed me; I was sick, and you visited me; I was in prison, and you came unto me." Then shall the righteous answer Him saying, "Lord, when did we see you hungry and feed you? or thirsty and gave you a drink? When did we see you as a stranger, and take you in? or naked and clothed you? Or when did we see you sick, or in prison, and come visit you?" And the King shall answer and say unto them, "Verily, I say unto you, inasmuch as you have done it unto one of the least of these my brethren, you have done it unto me." Then shall He say also unto them on the left hand, "Depart from me, ye cursed, into everlasting fire, prepared for the devil and his angels: for I was hungry, and you gave me no meat. I was thirsty, and you gave me no drink. I was a stranger, and you took me not in; naked, and you clothed me not; sick and in prison, and you visited me not." Then they shall also answer Him saying, "Lord, when did we see you hungry, or thirsty, or a stranger, or naked, or sick, or in prison, and did not minister to you?" Then He shall answer them saying, "Verily I say unto you, inasmuch as you did it not unto one of the least of these, you did it not to me." And these shall go away into everlasting punishment: but the righteous into life eternal.[4]

A new commandment I give unto you, that you love one another; as I have loved you, that you also love one another.[5]

References:

1) James 2:15-17 2) Mark 9:41 3) James 4:17
4) Matthew 25:34-46 5) John 13:34

What The Bible Says About . . .
PAYING TAXES

How Jesus Handled The Tax Question:
After Jesus and his disciples arrived in
Capernaum, the collectors of the half-shekel
tax came to Peter and said, "Doesn't your
master pay taxes?" "Yes, He does", Peter
replied. But when Peter came into the house,
Jesus spoke up first and said, "What do you
think, Simon? Of whom do the kings of the
earth take toll or tribute? Of their own
children or of strangers?" Peter said, "Of
strangers." Jesus then said, "Then are the
children free. However, lest we should
offend them, go to the sea and cast a hook,
and take up the first fish, and when you
open his mouth, you will find a piece of
money. That take, and give unto them for
me and you."[1]

"Tell us therefore, what thinkest thou? Is it
lawful to give tribute unto Caesar, or not?"
But Jesus perceived their wickedness and
said, "Why tempt ye me, you hypocrites?
Show me the tribute money." And they
brought Him a penny. And He said unto
them, "Whose is this image and superscrip-
tion?" They said unto Him, "Caesar's."

Then said He unto them, "Render therefore unto Caesar the things which are Caesar's; and unto God the things that are God's."[2]

The Apostle Paul's Comments: Let every soul be subject unto the higher powers, for there is no power but of God. Whosoever therefore resists the power, resists the ordinance of God; and they that resist shall receive to themselves damnation. For rulers are not a terror to good works, but to the evil. Wilt thou then not be afraid of the power? Do that which is good, and thou shalt have praise of the same: for he is the minister of God to thee for good. But if you do that which is evil, be afraid; for he beareth not the sword in vain: for he is the minister of God, a revenger to execute wrath upon him that does evil. Wherefore you must needs be subject, not only for wrath, but also for conscience sake. For this cause, you pay tribute also: for they are God's ministers, attending continually upon this very thing. Render therefore to all their dues: tribute to whom tribute is due; custom to whom custom; fear to whom fear; honor to whom honor.[3]

References:

1) Matthew 17:24-27 2) Matthew 22:17-21
3) Romans 13:1-7

CHAPTER 78

What The Bible Says About . . .
HIRING NEW EMPLOYEES

Know them which labor among you,[1] and be not unequally yoked together with unbelievers: for what fellowship has righteousness with unrighteousness? And what communion has light with darkness?[2] Withdraw yourself from every brother that walks disorderly.[3]

He that is slothful makes excuses not to work[4] and is a brother to him that is a great waster.[5] A sluggard won't even work when it's cold; therefore, shall he beg in harvest and have nothing.[6]

Don't let him that works deceit dwell in your house, or he that tells lies tarry in your sight.[7] In all labor there is profit,[8] but the labor of the righteous tends toward life,[9] and mere talk leads only to poverty.[8]

There is more hope of a fool, than in a man who is wise in his own conceit;[10] and he that has no self control is like a city whose walls are broken down.[11]

Confidence in an unfaithful man in time of

troubles is like a broken tooth, and a foot out of joint,[12] but as for the pure, his work is right.[13]

References:

1) I Thessalonians 5:12 2) II Corinthians 6:14
3) II Thessalonians 3:6 4) Proverbs 22:13
5) Proverbs 18:9 6) Proverbs 20:4 7) Psalms 101:7
8) Proverbs 14:23 9) Proverbs 10:16
10) Proverbs 26:12 11) Proverbs 25:28
12) Proverbs 25:19 13) Proverbs 21:8

CHAPTER 79

What The Bible Says About . . .

CORRECTING A SUBORDINATE

A reproof will enter more into a wise man than a hundred stripes into a fool,[1] and he that refuses instruction despises his own soul: but he that hears reproof gets understanding.[2]

And you masters, give unto your servants that which is just and equal,[3] forbearing threatening; knowing that your master also is in heaven; neither is there respect of persons with Him.[4]

Reprove not a scorner, lest he hate you: but rebuke a wise man, and he will love you.[5] He that has knowledge spares his words,[6] and an open rebuke is better than secret love.[7] Correction is grievous unto him that forsakes the way: and he that hates reproof shall die.[8] Now no chastening for the present seems to be joyous, but grievous: nevertheless, afterward it yields the peaceable fruit of righteousness to those who have been trained by it,[9] but he that refuses reproof erreth[10] and is brutish.[11] In fact, poverty and shame will come to him that refuses instruction,[12] but he that regards reproof is prudent[13] and shall be honored.[12]

Remember that he that hears the reproof of life abides among the wise.[14]

References:

1) Proverbs 17:10 2) Proverbs 15:32
3) Colossians 4:1 4) Ephesians 6:9
5) Proverbs 9:8 6) Proverbs 17:27
7) Proverbs 27:5 8) Proverbs 15:10
9) Hebrews 12:11 10) Proverbs 10:17
11) Proverbs 12:1 12) Proverbs 13:18
13) Proverbs 15:5 14) Proverbs 15:31

CHAPTER 80

What The Bible Says About . . .

DRESS CODE

The woman shall not wear that which pertains to a man, nor shall a man wear women's clothing; for all who do these things are an abomination unto the Lord.[1] Women should adorn themselves in modest apparel, with decency and propriety. Christian women should be noticed for their good works, not for the way they fix their hair or because of their gold jewelry, pearls or expensive clothing.[2] Their adorning should not be merely external, but let it be the hidden man of the heart, in that which is not corruptible, even the ornament of a meek and quiet spirit, which is in the sight of God of great price. For after this manner in the old time the holy women also, who trusted in God, adorned themselves, being in subjection unto their own husbands.[3]

Finally brethren, judge not according to the appearance, but judge righteous judgement.[4]

References:

*1) Deuteronomy 22:5 2) I Timothy 2:9,10
3) I Peter 3:3-5 4) John 7:24*

CHAPTER 81

What The Bible Says About . . .

PARTNERSHIPS

Be ye not unequally yoked together with unbelievers: for what fellowship has righteousness with unrighteousness? And what communion has light with darkness?[1] And whoever is partner with a thief hates his own soul.[2] Also, can two walk together except they be agreed?[3]

That if two of you shall agree on earth as touching anything that they shall ask, it shall be done for them of My Father which is in heaven.[4] Two are better than one because they have a good reward for their labor. For if they fall, the one will lift up his fellow: but woe to him that is alone when he falls; for he doesn't have another to help him up. Again, if two lie together, then they have heat: but how can one be warm alone? And if one prevail against him, two shall withstand him, and a threefold cord is not quickly broken.[5]

Now, I beseech you brethren, by the name of our Lord Jesus Christ, that you speak the same thing, and let there be no divisions among you; but that you be perfectly joined together in the same mind and in the same judgment.[6]

Whether any do enquire of Titus, he is my partner and fellow helper concerning you: or our brethren be enquired of, they are the messengers of the churches, and the glory of Christ.[7] If you count me therefore a partner, receive him as myself.[8] And they beckoned unto their partners, which were in the other ship, that they should come and help them. And they came, and filled both the ships, so that they began to sink.[9] And so was also James, and John, the sons of Zebedee, which were partners with Simon. And Jesus said unto Simon, "Fear not; from henceforth, you shall catch men."[10]

References:

1) II Corinthians 6:14 2) Proverbs 29:24 3) Amos 3:3
4) Matthew 18:19 5) Ecclesiastes 4:9-12
6) I Corinthians 1:10 7) II Corinthians 8:23
8) Philemon 1:17 9) Luke 5:7 10) Luke 5:10

SECTION III

EXPERIENCING GOD'S LOVE IN A TROUBLED WORLD

CHAPTER 82

YOUR NEED FOR GOD

Wherefore, as by one man (Adam), sin entered into the world, and death by sin; and so death passed upon all men,[1] for all have sinned and fallen short of God's glory.[2] All we like sheep have gone astray; we have turned every one to his own way.[3] We have all become like an unclean thing, and all our righteous acts are like filthy rags.[4] For the wages of sin is death, but the gift of God is eternal life through Jesus Christ our Lord.[5]

But God demonstrated His love for us, in that, while we were yet sinners, Christ died for us.[6] And this is the condemnation, that light is come into the world, and men loved darkness rather than light, because their deeds were evil;[7] and whoever denies Jesus before men, Jesus will also deny him before the Father which is in heaven.[8] And if you don't believe that Jesus is the Son of God, you will die in your sins.[9] Just believing that there is one God is not good enough; the devils believe that, and shudder in terror.[10]

Remember, he that has the Son has life; and

he that has not the Son of God, has not life.[11]

References:

1) Romans 5:12 2) Romans 3:23 3) Isaiah 53:6
4) Isaiah 64:6 5) Romans 6:23 6) Romans 5:8
7) John 3:19 8) Matthew 10:33 9) John 8:24
10) James 2:19 11) I John 5:12

CHAPTER 83

EXPERIENCING GOD'S FORGIVENESS FOR THE FIRST TIME

Behold, I stand at the door and knock: if any man hear My voice, and open the door, I will come in to him, and will sup with him, and he with Me.[1]

For God loved the world so much that He gave His only Son, that whoever believes in Him should not perish, but have life everlasting. For God didn't send His Son into the world to condemn it; but that the world through Him might be saved.[2] You see, Christ died for our sins according to the scriptures; and He was buried and rose again as the scriptures foretold He would.[3] And if you confess with your mouth the Lord Jesus, and believe in your heart that God has raised Him from the dead, you will be saved. For with the heart man believes unto righteousness; and with the mouth confession is made unto salvation;[4] and as many as receive Jesus, to them He gives power to become the sons of God.[5]

He that spared not His own Son, but delivered Him up for us all, how shall He not with Him also, freely give us all things?[6] Let us therefore come boldly unto the throne of grace, that we may obtain mercy, and find grace to help in time of need.[7] And if we confess our sins, He is faithful and just to forgive us our sins, and to cleanse us from all unrighteousness.[8]

And this is the record, that God has given to us eternal life, and this life is in His Son.[9] Whosoever therefore shall confess Jesus before men, Jesus will confess him before the Father which is in heaven.[10] These things have I written unto you that believe on the name of the Son of God; that you may know that you have eternal life, and that you may believe on the name of the Son of God.[11]

References:

1) Revelation 3:20 2) John 3:16,17 3) I Corinthians 15:3,4
4) Romans 10:9,10 5) John 1:12 6) Romans 8:32
7) Hebrews 4:16 8) I John 1:9 9) I John 5:11
10) Matthew 10:32 11) I John 5:13

CHAPTER 84

WHO JESUS IS

Wherefore God also has highly exalted Him, and given Him a name which is above every name: that at the name of Jesus every knee should bow, of things in heaven, and things in earth, and things under the earth; and that every tongue should confess that Jesus Christ is Lord, to the glory of God the Father.[1] The Father[2] sent Jesus, the Son of God,[3] to be the Savior of the world.[2] He is the Son of man come to seek and to save that which was lost.[4] He is the Christ,[5] the only begotten Son of the Father[6] who came to dwell in our hearts[7] and load us daily with benefits.[8]

If we love Him and keep His commandments, He will love us, and manifest Himself to us.[9] He is absolutely Wonderful, a Counsellor, The Mighty God, The Everlasting Father, The Prince of Peace,[10] and the Lord Jesus Christ.[11] He will be merciful to your unrighteousness and your sins and iniquities He will remember no more.[12] He is the way, the truth, and the life, the only way to the Father.[13] He preaches the gospel to the poor, and heals the brokenhearted. He preaches deliverance to the captives, and recovering of sight to the blind. He sets at liberty them that are bruised,[14] and heals all our diseases.[15]

He is light, and in Him is no darkness at all.[16] He redeems your life from destruction, crowns you with lovingkindness and tender mercies, satisfies your mouth with good things, so that your youth is renewed like the eagles,[17] and cleanses us from all sin.[18]

He made Himself of no reputation, and took upon Him the form of a servant, and was made in the likeness of men: and being found in fashion as a man, He humbled Himself, and became obedient unto death, even the death of the cross,[19] and became the author and finisher of our faith.[20]

He is a friend that sticks closer than a brother[21] and promises to never leave us nor forsake us.[22] Draw close to Him, and He will draw close to you.[23] He is the firstborn among many brethren, a shield, our glory, and the lifter of our heads.[24] He is the bread of life, so you won't have to hunger or thirst.[25] He is the great I AM[26] and the door of the sheep[27] providing you green pastures[28] and still waters.[29] He is the Good Shepherd and gives His life for the sheep.[30] He came as a light into this world, so we wouldn't have to be in darkness.[31] He is the resurrection and the life, so we can live.[32] Jesus is the true vine, His Father is the gardener, and we are the branches, living for Him to bring forth much fruit.[33]

References:

1) Philippians 2:9,10 2) I John 4:14
3) I John 4:15 4) Luke 19:10 5) John 4:42
6) John 3:16 7) Ephesians 3:17 8) Psalms 68:19
9) John 14:21 10) Isaiah 9:6 11) Romans 16:20
12) Hebrews 8:12 13) John 14:6 14) Luke 4:18
15) Psalms 103:3 16) I John 1:5 17) Psalms 103:4,5
18) I John 1:7 19) Philippians 2:7,8 20) Hebrews 12:2
21) Proverbs 18:24 22) Hebrews 13:5 23) James 4:8
24) Psalms 3:3 25) John 6:35 26) John 8:58
27) John 10:7 28) John 10:9 29) Psalms 23:2
30) John 10:11 31) John 12:46 32) John 11:25
33) John 15:5

CHAPTER 85

UNDERSTANDING THE HOLY GHOST

Jesus said, "I will pray the Father, and He will give you another Comforter, that He may abide with you forever; even the Spirit of truth; whom the world cannot receive, because it cannot see Him; neither does it know Him; but you know Him; for He dwells with you, and shall be in you.[1] When the Comforter is come, He shall testify of Me[2] and guide you into all truth: for He shall not speak of Himself, but whatever He hears, that will He speak: and He will show you things to come. He shall glorify Me: for He shall receive of Mine, and declare it to you.[3] Nevertheless, I tell you the truth; it is expedient for you that I go away: for if I do not go away, the Comforter will not come unto you; but if I depart, I will send Him to you.[4] He that believes on Me, as the scripture has said, out of his belly shall flow rivers of living water. (But this spoke He of the Spirit, which they that believe on Him should receive: for the Holy Ghost was not yet given because Jesus was not yet glorified.)[5]

And when they bring you unto the synagogues, and unto magistrates, and powers, take no thought how or what you shall answer: for the Holy Ghost shall teach you in the same hour what you ought to say.[6]

But you shall receive power, after the Holy Ghost is come upon you; and you shall be witnesses to the uttermost parts of the earth,[7] and the Spirit will bring everything Jesus said to your remembrance.[8]

New Testament Examples of Receiving the Holy Spirit:

1. And when the day of Pentecost was fully come, they were all with one accord in one place. And suddenly there came a sound from heaven as of a rushing mighty wind, and it filled all the house where they were sitting. And there appeared unto them cloven tongues like as of fire, and it sat upon each of them. And they were all filled with the Holy Ghost, and began to speak with other tongues, as the Spirit gave them utterance.[9]

2. And when they had prayed, the place was shaken where they were assembled together; and they were all filled with the Holy Ghost, and they spoke the word of God with boldness.[10]

3. Now then the apostles which were at Jerusalem heard that Samaria had received the word of God, they sent unto them Peter and John, who, when they were come down, prayed for them, that they might receive the Holy Ghost: (for as yet He was fallen on none of them: only they were baptized in the name of the Lord Jesus). Then they laid their hands on them, and they received the Holy Ghost.[11]

4. While Peter yet spoke these words, the Holy Ghost fell on all them which heard the word. And they of the circumcision which believed were astonished, as many as came with Peter, because that on the Gentiles also was poured out the gift of the Holy Ghost. For they heard them speak with tongues, and magnify God. Then answered Peter, "Can any man forbid water, that these should not be baptized, which have received the Holy Ghost as well as we?"[12]

5. And it came to pass, that, while Apollos was at Corinth, Paul having passed through the upper coasts came to Ephesus: and finding certain disciples, he said unto them, "Have you received the Holy Ghost since you believed?" And they said unto him, "We have not so much as heard whether there be any Holy Ghost." And he said unto them, "Unto what then were you baptized?" And

they said, "Unto John's baptism." Then Paul said, "John verily baptized with the baptism of repentance, saying unto the people, that they should believe on Him which should come after him, that is, on Christ Jesus." When they heard this, they were baptized in the name of Jesus; and when Paul laid his hands upon them, the Holy Ghost came on them; and they spake with tongues, and prophesied.[13]

If you then, being evil, know how to give good gifts to your children: how much more shall your heavenly Father give the Holy Spirit to them that ask Him?[14] Your body is the temple of the Holy Ghost,[15] so build yourself up on your most holy faith, praying in the Holy Ghost.[16]

Be not drunk with wine wherein is excess; but be filled with the Spirit;[17] and as many as are led by the Spirit of God, they are the sons of God.[18] For what man knows the things of a man, save the spirit of man which is in him? Even so, the things of God are known by no man, but the Spirit of God. Now we have received, not the spirit of the world, but the Spirit which is of God; that we might know the things that are freely given to us of God.[19] Only grieve not the Holy Spirit of God, whereby you are sealed unto the day of redemption.[20]

References:

1) John 14:16-17 2) John 15:26 3) John 16:13-14
4) John 16:7 5) John 7:38-39 6) Luke 12:11-12
7) Acts 1:8 8) John 14:26 9) Acts 2:1–4 10) Acts 4:31
11) Acts 8:14–17 12) Acts 10:44–47 13) Acts 19:1–6
14) Luke 11:13 15) I Corinthians 6:19 16) Jude 1:20
17) Ephesians 5:18 18) Romans 8:14
19) I Corinthians 2:11-12 20) Ephesians 4:30

CHAPTER 86

TRUSTING GOD

Trust in the Lord with all your heart, lean not unto your own understanding. In all your ways acknowledge Him, and He will direct your paths.[1] Yes, trust in God who is your rock,[2] for His way is perfect, His word is tried and true, and He is a buckler to all that trust in Him.[3]

Let everyone who puts their trust in God rejoice and ever shout for joy, because he defends them,[4] He is their shield and the horn of their salvation.[2] They that know His name will trust in God, for He has not forsaken them that seek Him,[5] for He saves with His right hand those who put their trust in Him, from those that rise up against them.[6]

Yes, the Lord is my rock, and my fortress, and my deliverer, my high tower, my God, my strength in whom I will trust.[7] He saves me from violence, and is my refuge and Savior.[2] Although some trust in chariots and some in horses, we will remember the name of the Lord our God,[8] for He redeems the souls of His servants so that none that trust in Him shall be desolate.[9]

The Lord is good, a stronghold in the day of trouble, and He knows them that trust in Him;[10] they will not be ashamed, nor will their enemies triumph over them.[11] In fact, they that trust in the Lord and do good shall dwell in the land, and be fed,[12] prosperous,[13] blessed[14] and safe,[15] and whatever they have committed to the Lord, He will bring it to pass.[16]

It is better to trust in the Lord than to put confidence in man.[17] Do not be afraid of what man can do to you,[18] for the fear of man brings a snare,[15] but those who trust under His wings will He cover with His feathers, and His truth will be a shield and buckler to them.[19]

When you are afraid, trust in God,[20] who raises the dead[21] and causes you to possess the land, and inherit His holy mountain.[22] Do not trust in uncertain riches, but in the living God, who gives us richly all things to enjoy.[23] Those who do trust in riches have a very hard time entering in to the kingdom of God.[24]

The man that makes his trust in the Lord, not respecting the proud or turning aside to lies will be blessed[25] and trust in the mercy of God forever and ever.[26]

References:

1) Proverbs 3:5,6 2) II Samuel 22:3
3) II Samuel 22:31 4) Psalms 5:11
5) Psalms 9:10 6) Psalms 17:7 7) Psalms 18:2
8) Psalms 20:7 9) Psalms 34:22 10) Nahum 1:7
11) Psalms 25:2 12) Psalms 37:3 13) Proverbs 28:25
14) Psalms 2:12 15) Proverbs 29:25
16) Psalms 37:5 17) Psalms 118:8
18) Psalms 56:11 19) Psalms 91:4
20) Psalms 56:3 21) II Corinthians 1:9
22) Isaiah 57:13 23) I Timothy 6:17
24) Mark 10:24 25) Psalms 40:4
26) Psalms 52:8

CHAPTER 87

PRAYER

Men ought always to pray, and not to faint.[1]
Pray without ceasing,[2] yes, pray that you
enter not into temptation,[3] pray for the
peace of Jerusalem,[4] pray for them which
despitefully use you and persecute you,[5]
pray that the Lord of the harvest will send
forth laborers into the harvest, [6] pray for the
sick,[7] pray for one another that you may be
healed,[8] pray that you may be accounted
worthy to escape all these things that shall
come to pass, and to stand before the Son of
man.[9] And when you don't know how to
pray, the Spirit will also help you in your
weakness, making intercession for you
with groanings which cannot be uttered.[10]
Build yourself up on your most holy faith,
praying in the Holy Ghost,[11] for when we
pray in an unknown tongue, our spirit prays,
though our understanding is unfruitful. So
pray with the Spirit and with your understanding also.[12]

Men everywhere ought to pray, lifting up
holy hands, without wrath and doubting,[13]
for he that is doubtful is like a wave of the
sea driven with the wind and tossed, Let not

that man think he shall receive anything of the Lord.[14] When you pray, you should not be as the hypocrites are: for they love to pray standing in the synagogues and in the corners of the streets, that they may be seen of men. Truly, they have their reward. But when you pray, enter into your closet, and when you have shut your door, pray to your Father which is in secret; and your Father which sees in secret will reward you openly. But when you pray, use not vain repetitions, as the heathen do: for they think that they shall be heard for their much speaking.[15] And when you stand praying, forgive, if you have ought against any, that your Father in heaven may also forgive you your trespasses.[16]

After this manner pray: Our Father, which is in heaven, hallowed be Thy name. Thy kingdom come, Thy will be done in earth as it is in heaven. Give us this day our daily bread, and forgive us our debts, as we forgive our debtors. And lead us not into temptation, but deliver us from evil: for Thine is the kingdom and the power, and the glory, forever. Amen.[17]

Biblical Examples of Prayer Habits:

1. And it came to pass in those days, that He went out into a mountain to pray, and continued all night in prayer to God.[18]

2. Evening, and morning, and at noon, will I pray, and cry aloud: and he shall hear my voice.[19]

3. And when He had sent the multitudes away, He went up into a mountain apart to pray: and when the evening was come, He was there alone.[20]

4. Epaphras, who is one of you, a servant of Christ, saluteth you, always labouring fervently for you in prayers, that ye may stand perfect and complete in all the will of God.[21]

5. Now when Daniel knew that the writing was signed, he went into his house; and his windows being open in his chamber toward Jerusalem, he kneeled upon his knees three times a day, and prayed, and gave thanks before his God, as he did aforetime.[22]

6. And in the morning, rising up a great while before day, He went out, and departed into a solitary place, and there prayed.[23]

7. And He withdrew Himself into the wilderness, and prayed.[24]

8. ...night and day praying exceedingly that we might see your face, and might perfect that which is lacking in your faith?[25]

9. ...a devout man, and one that feared God with all his house, which gave much alms to the people, and prayed to God always.[26]

The eyes of the Lord are over the righteous, and His ears are open unto their prayers.[27] Yes, the effectual fervent prayer of a righteous man avails much.[28] So, continue in prayer,[29] for we have this confidence in God, that if we ask anything according to His will, He hears us: and if we know that He hears us, whatsoever we ask, we know that we have the petitions that we desired of Him.[30] For everything that we ask in prayer, believing, we shall receive.[31]

The prayer of the upright is God's delight,[32] and he hears the prayer of the righteous,[33] and regards the prayer of the destitute and will not despise their prayer.[34] If God's people, which are called by His name, shall humble themselves, and pray, and seek His face, and turn from their wicked ways; then will He hear from heaven, and will forgive their sin, and will heal their land.[35]

Husbands should dwell with them according to knowledge, giving honor unto the wife, as unto the weaker vessel, and as being heirs together of the grace of life; that your prayers be not hindered.[36] Pray always with all prayer and supplication in the Spirit,[37]

256

being careful for nothing; but in everything by prayer and supplication with thanksgiving, let your requests be made known to God.[38] For the spirit indeed is willing, but the flesh is weak.[39] So, continue instant in prayer,[40] and fastings often,[41] knowing that what things you desire, when you pray, believe that you receive them, and you shall have them.[42]

References:

1) Luke 18:1 2) I Thessalonians 5:17 3) Luke 22:40
4) Psalms 122:6 5) Matthew 5:44 6) Matthew 9:38
7) James 5:13–14 8) James 5:16 9) Luke 21:36
10) Romans 8:26 11) Jude 1:20 12) I Corinthians 14:14–15
13) I Timothy 2:8 14) James 1:6–7 15) Matthew 6:5–7
16) Mark 11:25 17) Matthew 6:9–13 18) Luke 6:12
19) Psalms 55:17 20) Matthew 14:23 21) Colossians 4:12
22) Daniel 6:10 23) Mark 1:35 24) Luke 5:16
25) I Thessalonians 3:10 26) Acts 10:2 27) I Peter 3:12
28) James 5:16 29) Colossians 4:2
30) I John 5: 14–15 31) Matthew 21:22 32) Proverbs 15:8
33) Proverbs 15:29 34) Psalms 102:17
35) II Chronicles 7:14 36) I Peter 3:7 37) Ephesians 6:18
38) Philippians 4:6 39) Matthew 26:41 40) Romans 12:12
41) II Corinthians 11:27 42) Mark 11:24

CHAPTER 88

KNOWING GOD'S WILL

Wherefore, do not be unwise, but understand what the will of the Lord is.[1] Submit yourself to every ordinance of man for the Lord's sake; whether it be to the king as supreme, or unto governors, as unto them that are sent by Him for the punishment of evil doers, and for the praise of them that do well. For so is the will of God, that with well doing you may put to silence the ignorance of foolish men.[2]

Do the will of God from your heart,[3] and this is the will of God, even your sanctification, that you should abstain from fornication, that every one of you should know how to possess his vessel in sanctification and honor,[4] not in the lust of concupiscence, even as the Gentiles which know not God: that no man go beyond and defraud his brother in any matter: because the Lord is the avenger of all such, as we also have forewarned you and testified. For God has not called us unto uncleanness, but unto holiness. Therefore, whoever rejects this is not rejecting man, but God, who gave us the Holy Spirit.[5] In everything give thanks; for this is the will of God in Christ Jesus concerning you.[6]

If any man lack wisdom, let him ask of God that gives to all men liberally, without fault finding, and it shall be given him, only let him ask in faith.[7]

My son keep your father's commandment, forsake not the law of your mother; bind them continually upon your heart, and tie them around your neck. When you go, it shall lead you, when you sleep, it will keep you, and when you waken, it will talk with you. For the commandment is a lamp; and the law is light; and reproofs of instruction are the way of life.[8]

Trust in the Lord with all your heart; lean not unto your own understanding. In all your ways acknowledge Him, and He will direct your paths.[9] Yes, commit your works unto the Lord, and your thoughts will be established.[10] Our God will be our guide even unto death.[11] His word is a lamp unto our feet and a light unto our path.[12] He gave us His good spirit to instruct us,[13] therefore for His name's sake He will lead us and guide us.[14]

Not everyone that says, 'Lord, Lord,' shall enter into the kingdom of heaven; but he that does the will of the Father which is in heaven.[15] For whosoever shall do the will of the Father in heaven, the same is the brother, sister or mother of Jesus.[16] So live your life to do the will of God, and not in the flesh to the lusts of men.[17]

The Lord will instruct you and teach you in the way you should go. He will guide you with His eye,[18] and your ears shall hear a word behind you saying, 'This is the way, walk ye in it,' when you turn to the right hand and when you turn to the left.[19] The steps of a good man are ordered by the Lord, and He delights in each step he takes,[20] for He is the Lord your God, which teaches you to profit, and leads you by the way you should go.[21] And the Lord will guide you continually,[22] leading you with His hand[23] in truth[24] on a plain path,[25] satisfying your soul in drought, making fat your bones: and you will be like a watered garden, and like a spring of water, whose waters fail not.[22]

Howbeit when He, the Spirit of truth, is come, He will guide you into all truth: for He shall not speak of Himself, but whatever He hears, that will He speak; and He will show you things to come.[26] And He that searches the hearts knows what is the mind of the Spirit, because He makes intercession for the saints according to the will of God.[27]

And be not conformed to this world; but be transformed by the renewing of your mind, that you may prove what is that good and acceptable, and perfect will of God.[28] And after you have done the will of God, you will receive the promise,[29] and he that does the will of God abides forever.[30]

References:

1) Ephesians 5:17 2) I Peter 2:13-15
3) Ephesians 6:6 4) I Thessalonians 4:3,4
5) I Thessalonians 4:5-8 6) I Thessalonians 5:18
7) James 1:5,6 8) Proverbs 6:20-23
9) Proverbs 3:5, 6 10) Proverbs 16:3
11) Psalms 48:14 12) Psalms 119:105
13) Nehemiah 9:20 14) Psalms 31:3
15) Matthew 7:21 16) Matthew 12:50
17) I Peter 4:2 18) Psalms 32:8 19) Isaiah 30:21
20) Psalms 37:23 21) Isaiah 48:17 22) Isaiah 58:11
23) Psalms 139:10 24) Psalms 25:5 25) Psalms 27:11
26) John 16:13 27) Romans 8:27 28) Romans 12:2
29) Hebrews 10:36 30) I John 2:17

CHAPTER 89

DISCERNMENT

Whoso keepeth the commandment shall feel no evil thing: and a wise man's heart discerneth both time and judgement.[1] The natural man receives not the things of the Spirit of God: for they are foolishness unto him: neither can he know them, because they are spiritually discerned. But he that is spiritual judgeth all things, yet he himself is judged of no man.[2] Strong meat belongs to them that are of full age, even those who by reason of use have their senses exercised to discern both good and evil.[3]

Let a man examine himself, and so let him eat of that bread, and drink of that cup. For he that eats and drinks unworthily, eats and drinks damnation to himself, not discerning the Lord's body. For this cause many are weak and sickly among you, and many sleep.[4]

Let Christ dwell in your heart by faith, that you being rooted and grounded in love, may be able to comprehend with all saints what is the breadth, and length and depth and height; and to know the love of Christ, which passeth knowledge that you might be filled with all the fullness of God.[5]

Remember that the word of God is quick and powerful and sharper than any two edged sword, piercing even to the dividing asunder of soul and spirit and of the joints and marrow and is a discerner of the thoughts and intents of the heart.[6] So study that you may know wisdom and instruction to perceive the words of understanding.[7]

References:

1) Ecclesiastes 8:5   2) I Corinthians 2:14,15
3) Hebrews 5:14   4) I Corinthians 11:28-30
5) Ephesians 3:17-19   6) Hebrews 4:12
7) Proverbs 1:2

CHAPTER 90

GOD'S CARING CORRECTION

Behold, God has set before you blessing and a curse; a blessing, if you obey the commandments of the Lord your God, which He commands you: and a curse if you will not obey the commandments of the Lord your God, but turn aside out of the way which He commands you, to go after other gods, which you have not known.[1]

Don't despise the chastening of the Lord; neither be weary of His correction,[2] for whom the Lord loveth, He correcteth; even as a father the son in whom He delighteth.[3] As a man chasteneth his son, so the Lord thy God chasteneth thee,[4] so don't despise it when it happens or faint when you are rebuked of Him; for whom the Lord loveth, He chasteneth and scourgeth every son whom He receives. If you endure chastening, God deals with you as with sons; for what son is he whom the Father chastens not? But if you are not chastised, whereof all are partakers, then are you bastards, and not sons. Furthermore, when our fathers of the flesh corrected us, we gave them reverence:

shall we not much rather be in subjection unto the Father of spirits and live? For they for a few days chastened us after their own pleasure; but He for our profit, that we might be partakers of His holiness. Now no chastening for the present seems to be joyous, but grievous: nevertheless afterward it yieldeth the peaceable fruit of right-eousness unto them which are exercised thereby.[5]

Blessed and happy is the man whom God corrects[6] and chastens.[7] Therefore, despise not the chastening of the Almighty,[6] and let Him teach you out of His law,[7] for all scripture is given by inspiration of God, and is profit-able for doctrine, for reproof, for correction, and for instruction in righteousness.[8]

As many as God loves, He rebukes and chastens,[9] but when we are judged, we are chastened of the Lord, so we won't be con-demned with the world.[10] But remember, obedience is better than sacrifice.[11]

References:

1) Deuteronomy 11:26-28 2) Proverbs 3:11
3) Proverbs 3:12 4) Deuteronomy 8:5 5) Hebrews 12:5-11
6) Job 5:17 7.Psalms 94:12 8) II Timothy 3:16
9) Revelation 3:19 10) I Corinthians 11:32
11) I Samuel 15:22

CHAPTER 91

GOD'S ASSISTANCE

The Lord thinks on you; He is your deliverer,[1] your strength,[2] your shield,[3] your refuge and a very present help in trouble[2] if you will wait for Him,[3] trust in Him,[4] and choose His precepts.[5] Your help comes from God,[6] and is in the name of the Lord, who made heaven and earth.[7]

Fear not, for God is with you; be not dismayed for He is your God; He will strengthen you; yes, He will help you; yes, He will uphold you with the right hand of His righteousness.[8] Yes, fear not, for the Lord your God will hold your right hand, and say unto you, "Fear not; I will help you."[9]

The angel of the Lord will go before you,[10] encamp round about you,[11] make the crooked places straight,[12] and the Lord will be with you, never failing you, neither forsaking you, so fear not, neither be dismayed,[13] for the battle is not yours, but God's.[14]

Come boldly unto the throne of grace, that you may obtain mercy, and find grace to help in time of need;[15] and the Holy Ghost shall teach you in the same hour what you ought to say.[16]

The meek will He guide in judgment: and the meek will He teach His way.[17] He shall guide you with counsel[18] and instruct you and teach you in the way which you should go. He will guide you with His eye[19] and afterward receive you to glory.[18] Howbeit when He, the Spirit of truth, is come, He will guide you into all truth: for He shall not speak of Himself; but whatsoever He shall hear, that shall He speak: and He will show you things to come.[20]

References:

*1) Psalms 40:17   2) Psalms 46:1   3) Psalms 33:20
4) Psalms 37:40   5) Psalms 119:173   6) Psalms 121:2
7) Psalms 124:8   8) Isaiah 41:10   9) Isaiah 41:13
10) Exodus 32:34   11) Psalms 34:7   12) Isaiah 45:2
13) Deuteronomy 31:8   14) II Chronicles 20:15
15) Hebrews 4:16   16) Luke 12:12   17) Psalms 25:9
18) Psalms 73:24   19) Psalms 32:8   20) John 16:13*

CHAPTER 92

THE POWER
OF HIS WORD

The Word of God is quick, and powerful, and sharper than any two-edged sword, piercing even to the dividing asunder of soul and spirit, and of the joints and marrow, and is a discerner of the thoughts and intents of the heart.[1] Through faith we understand that the worlds were framed by the Word of God, so that things which are seen were not made of things which do appear.[2]

In the beginning was the Word, and the Word was with God, and the Word was God.[3] All things were made by Him; and without Him was not anything made that was made. In Him was life; and the life was the light of men.[4] And the Word was made flesh, and dwelt among us, (and we beheld His glory, the glory as of the only begotten of the Father), full of grace and truth.[5] And the world was astonished at His doctrine: for His word was with power,[6] by speaking the word only, many were healed,[7] and spirits cast out.[8]

The entrance of His word gives light; and understanding to the simple.[9] It is a lamp to your feet, and a light for your path.[10] In His word we should hope[11] and trust,[12] for it is settled in heaven,[13] and even when heaven and earth pass away, His words shall not pass away.[14] He has magnified His word above His name,[15] and when it goes forth out of His mouth, it will not return void, but it will accomplish that which He pleases, and it will prosper in the thing where He sends it.[16] And He that executes God's word is strong,[17] and in knowing their God, they will do exploits,[18] for His word is truth[19] and very pure,[20] and it will stand forever.[21] Meditate in His word,[22] and it will strengthen you,[23] but he that despises the word shall be destroyed,[24] and his soul shall be utterly cut off.[25]

Let the word of Christ dwell in you richly in all wisdom,[26] for it is near you, even in your mouth, and in your heart: that is, the word of faith,[27] which sanctifies and cleanses you, like the washing of water.[28] Hold forth the word of life,[29] keeping the word of reconciliation,[30] which is the engrafted word and able to save your soul.[31] But be doers of the word, and not hearers only, deceiving your own selves.[32]

Man does not live by bread alone, but by

every word that proceeds out of the mouth of the Lord,[33] who upholds all things by the word of His power.[34] His word is tried and true,[35] and in sending His word, He healed them.[36] By the word of the Lord were the heavens made.[37] His word is right[38] and endures forever.[39] In fact, faith comes by hearing, and hearing by the word of God.[40]

So desire the sincere milk of the word, that you may grow,[41] taking heed thereto,[42] hiding it in your heart, that you might not sin against God.[43] For the gospel of Christ is the power of God unto salvation to every one that believes.[44]

References:

1) Hebrews 4:12 2) Hebrews 11:3 3) John 1:1
4) John 1:3,4 5) John 1:14 6) Luke 4:32 7) Matthew 8:8
8) Matthew 8:16 9) Psalms 119:130 10) Psalms 119:105
11) Psalms 119:81 12) Psalms 119:42 13) Psalms 119:89
14) Matthew 24:35 15) Psalms 138:2 16) Isaiah 55:11
17) Joel 2:11 18) Daniel 11:32 19) John 17:19
20) Psalms 119:140 21) Isaiah 40:8 22) Psalms 119:148
23) Psalms 119:28 24) Proverbs 13:13 25) Numbers 15:31
26) Colossians 3:16 27) Romans 10:8 28) Ephesians 5:26
29) Philippians 2:16 30) II Corinthians 5:19
31) James 1:21 32) James 1:22 33) Deuteronomy 8:3
34) Hebrews 1:3 35) II Samuel 22:31 36) Psalms 107:20
37) Psalms 33:6 38) Psalms 33:4 39) I Peter 1:25
40) Romans 10:17 41) I Peter 2:2 42) Psalms 119:9
43) Psalms 119:11 44) Romans 1:16

CHAPTER 93

THE POWER OF YOUR WORDS

Death and life are in the power of the tongue; and they that love it shall eat the fruit thereof.[1] A soft answer turns away wrath: but grievous words stir up anger.[2] You are snared by the words of your mouth, you are taken with the words of your mouth.[3]

Whosoever shall say unto this mountain, 'Be thou removed, and be cast into the sea', and shall not doubt in his heart, but shall believe that those things which he says shall come to pass, he shall have whatsoever he says.[4] In fact, if you had faith like a grain of mustard seed, you might say unto this sycamine tree, 'Be thou plucked up by the root, and be planted in the sea', and it would obey you.[5]

If you confess with your mouth the Lord Jesus, and shall believe in your heart that God has raised Him from the dead, you will be saved. For with the heart man believes unto righteousness, and with the mouth confession is made unto salvation.[6] So let us hold fast the profession of our faith without wavering; for he is faithful that promised.[7]

Let the weak say, 'I am strong';[8] wherefore comfort one another with these words.[9] If you abide in Christ, and His words abide in you, you shall ask what you will, and it shall be done unto you.[10]

The words of a man's mouth are a deep waters, and the wellspring of wisdom as a flowing brook.[11] The wise in heart shall be called prudent: and the sweetness of the lips increase learning.[12] A fool's mouth is his destruction, and his lips are the snare of his soul.[13] Pleasant words are like honeycomb, sweet to the soul, and health to the bones;[14] but a violent man uses his lips to bring evil to pass.[15]

Every idle word that men shall speak, they shall give account of in the day of judgment.[16] So let the words of your mouth and the meditation of your heart, be acceptable in God's sight.[17] For by your words you shall be justified, and by your words you shall be condemned.[18]

References:

1) Proverbs 18:21 2) Proverbs 15:1 3) Proverbs 6:2
4) Mark 11:23 5) Luke 17:6 6) Romans 10:8–9
7) Hebrews 10:23 8) Joel 3:10 9) I Thessalonians 4:18
10) John 15:7 11) Proverbs 18:4 12) Proverbs 16:21
13) Proverbs 18:7 14) Proverbs 16:24
15) Proverbs 16:29–30 16) Matthew 12:36
17) Psalms 19:14 18) Matthew 12:37

CHAPTER 94

SPIRITUAL AUTHORITY

Do not be ashamed of the gospel of Christ: for it is the power of God unto salvation to every one that believes.[1] As many as receive Jesus, He gives power to become sons of God, to them that believe on His name.[2] For Jesus became sin for us, who knew no sin; that we may be made the righteousness of God in Him.[3]

Jesus lives in believers, and the Father lives in Him[4] with all the fullness of the Godhead,[5] making us complete in Him.[6] And we know that we live in Him, and He in us, because He has given us of His spirit.[7] Let us therefore come boldly to the throne of grace, that we may obtain mercy, and find grace to help in time of need.[8] For He is able to do exceeding, abundantly above all that we ask or think, according to the power that works in us.[9]

But you shall receive power, after the Holy Ghost is come upon you; and you shall be witnesses unto Jesus unto the uttermost parts of the earth;[10] and the God of hope will fill you with all joy and peace in believing, that you may abound in hope, through the power of the Holy Ghost.[11] The night is far spent, the day is at hand: let us therefore cast off the works of darkness, and let us put on the armor of light,[12] being strong in the Lord, in the power of His might. Yes, put on the whole armor of God, that you may be able to stand against the schemes of the devil. For we wrestle not against flesh and blood, but against principalities, against powers, against the rulers of the darkness of this world, against spiritual wickedness in high places. Wherefore, take on the whole armor of God that you may be able to withstand in the evil day, and having done all, to stand. Stand therefore, with your loins girt about with truth, and having on the breastplate of righteousness; and your feet shod with the preparation of the gospel of peace. Above all, taking the shield of faith wherewith you will be able to quench all the fiery darts of the wicked; and take the helmet of salvation, and the sword of the spirit, which is the word of God.[13]

Give thanks to God, which gives us the victory through our Lord Jesus Christ,[14] making it possible to do all things through Christ who strengthens us,[15] because greater is He that is in me, than he that is in the world.[16] For though we walk in the flesh, we do not war after the flesh,[17] for the weapons

of our warfare are not carnal, but mighty
through God to the pulling down of strongholds; casting down imaginations and every
high thing that exalts itself against the
knowledge of God, and bringing into captivity every thought to the obedience of
Christ.[18]

You are no more a servant, but a son; and if a
son, then an heir of God through Christ.[19]
Therefore submit yourself to God. Resist the
devil, and he will flee from you.[20] For God
spoiled the powers and principalities, and
made an open show of them, triumphing
over them in it.[21]

Get to know Christ, and the power of His
resurrection, and the fellowship of His sufferings, being made comformable unto His
death,[22] strengthened with all might, according to His glorious power unto all patience,
with longsuffering and joyfulness.[23] For
God has not given us a spirit of fear: but of
power, and of love, and of a sound mind;[24]
that at the name of Jesus, every knee should
bow, of things in heaven, and things in
earth, and things under the earth.[25] And He
gave unto them power to tread upon serpents and scorpions, and over all the power
of the enemy: and nothing shall by any
means harm them.[26]

And what is the exceeding greatness of His power to usward who believe, according to the working of His mighty power, which he wrought in Christ, when He raised Him from the dead, and set Him at His own right hand in the heavenly places, far above all principality, and power, and might, and dominion, and every name that is named, not only in this world, but also in that which is to come: and has put all things under His feet, and gave Him to be the head over all things to the church, which is His body, the fullness of Him that filleth all in all.[27]

Turn away from those who have a form of godliness, but deny the power thereof,[28] for the kingdom of God is not in word, but in power;[29] and whatever you bind on earth, shall be bound in heaven, and whatever you loose on earth, shall be loosed in heaven. Again, if two of you shall agree on earth as touching anything that you will ask, it will be done for you by the Father which is in heaven.[30] For where two or more are gathered together in Jesus' name, He is there in the midst of them.[31]

References:

1) Romans 1:16 2) John 1:12 3) II Corinthians 5:21
4) John 17:23 5) Colossians 2:9 6) Colossians 2:10
7) I John 4:13 8) Hebrews 4:16 9) Ephesians 3:20
10) Acts 1:8 11) Romans 15:13 12) Romans 13:12
13) Ephesians 6:10-17 14) I Corinthians 15:57
15) Philippians 4:13 16) I John 4:4
17) II Corinthians 10:3 18) II Corinthians 10:4,5
19) Galatians 4:7 20) James 4:7 21) Colossians 2:15
22) Philippians 3:10 23) Colossians 1:11
24) II Timothy 1:7 25) Philippians 2:10
26) Luke 10:19 27) Ephesians 1:19-23
28) II Timothy 3:5 29) I Corinthians 4:20
30) Matthew 18:18,19 31) Matthew 18:20

CHAPTER 95

FAITH

Without faith it is impossible to please God: for he that comes to God must believe that He is, and that He is a rewarder of them that diligently seek Him.[1] Now faith comes by hearing and hearing by the word of God,[2] and is the substance of things hoped for, the evidence of things not seen.[3]

In times past, men of God, through faith subdued kingdoms, wrought righteousness, obtained promises, stopped the mouths of lions, quenched the violence of fire, escaped the edge of the sword, out of weakness were made strong, waxed valiant in fight, and turned to flight the armies of the aliens.[4]

Now we are justified by faith[5] and have access by faith into the grace wherein we stand, and rejoice in hope of the glory of God.[6] God has dealt to every man the measure of faith,[7] that we might become the children of God through faith in Jesus Christ.[8] For by grace are you saved through faith; and that not of yourselves: it is the gift of God.[9] Let us therefore come boldly to the throne of grace, that we may obtain mercy, and find grace to help in time of need:[10] that your faith should not stand in the wisdom of men, but in the power of God,[11] in whom we have boldness and access to God with confidence through faith in Christ.[12] So let us hold fast the profession of our faith without wavering; for He is faithful that promised.[13] Now the just shall live by faith: but if any man draws back, the Lord will have no pleasure in him.[14]

Through faith we understand that the worlds were framed by the word of God, so that things which are seen were not made of things which do appear.[15] So take the shield of faith, wherewith you shall be able to quench all the fiery darts of the wicked,[16] and the whole armor of God,[17] and fight the good fight of faith, laying hold of eternal life,[18] that Christ may dwell in your hearts by faith.[19]

You are kept by the power of God through faith unto salvation, though now for a season, if need be, you are in heaviness through many temptations - rejoice, for the trial of your faith is much more precious than gold which perishes.[20] For whatsoever is born of God overcomes the world; and this is the victory that overcomes the world, even our faith.[21] And the trying of your faith works patience, but let patience have her perfect work, that you may be perfect and entire, lacking nothing.[22]

If you have faith as a grain of mustard seed,[23] and doubt not, you shall not only do this which is done to the fig tree, but you shall say to the mountain, 'Be thou removed and cast into the sea,' and it shall be done,[24] and nothing shall be impossible to you.[23] Have faith in God,[25] and it will save you,[26] make you whole,[27] and what things you desire, when you pray, believe that you receive them, and you will have them.[28] If then God so clothes the grass, which is today in the field, and tomorrow is cast into the oven; how much more will He clothe you, O ye of little faith?[29]

Build yourself up on your most holy faith, by praying in the Holy Ghost,[30] for we walk by faith and not by sight,[31] and all things, whatsoever you shall ask in prayer, believing, you shall receive.[32] For the eyes of the Lord run to and fro throughout the whole earth, to show Himself strong in the behalf of them whose heart is perfect toward Him.[33]

Believe in the Lord your God, so shall you be established; believe His prophets, so shall you prosper.[34] Yes, if you can believe, all things are possible to him that believes.[35]

And these signs shall follow them that believe; in My name they shall cast out devils, speak with new tongues; pick up serpents safely; and if they drink any deadly thing, it won't hurt them; and they shall lay hands on the sick, and they shall recover.[36] And remember, faith, if it has not works, is dead.[37]

References:

1) Hebrews 11:6 2) Romans 10:17 3) Hebrews 11:1
4) Hebrews 11:33,34 5) Romans 5:1 6) Romans 5:2
7) Romans 12:3 8) Galatians 3:26 9) Ephesians 2:8
10) Hebrews 4:16 11) I Corinthians 2:5
12) Ephesians 3:12 13) Hebrews 10:23
14) Hebrews 10:38 15) Hebrews 11:3 16) Ephesians 6:16
17) Ephesians 6:13 18) I Timothy 6:12
19) Ephesians 3:17 20) I Peter 1:5-7 21) I John 5:4
22) James 1:3,4 23) Matthew 17:20 24) Matthew 21:21
25) Mark 11:22 26) Luke 7:50 27) Luke 8:48
28) Mark 11:24 29) Luke 12:28 30) Jude 1:20
31) II Corinthians 5:7 32) Matthew 21:22
33) II Chronicles 16:9 34) II Chronicles 20:20
35) Mark 9:23 36) Mark 16:17,18 37) James 2:17

CHAPTER 96

GOD'S COVENANT

Remember that you being in time past Gentiles in the flesh, who are called Uncircumcision by that which is called the Circumcision in the flesh made by hands; that at that time, you were without Christ, being aliens from the Commonwealth of Israel, and strangers from the covenants of promise, having no hope, and without God in the world: but now in Christ Jesus you who sometimes were far off are made near by the blood of Christ.[1]

Notable Covenants in the Bible:

1. I do set my bow in the cloud, and it shall be for a token of a covenant between me and the earth. And I will remember My covenant, which is between Me and you and every living creature of all flesh; and the waters shall no more become a flood to destroy all flesh. And the bow shall be in the cloud; and I will look upon it, that I may remember the everlasting covenant between God and every living creature of all flesh that is upon the earth.[2]

2. ...and said, "By Myself have I sworn," saith

the Lord, "for because thou hast done this thing, and hast not withheld thy son, thine only son: that in blessing I will bless thee, and in multiplying I will multiply thy seed as the stars of the heaven, and as the sand which is upon the sea shore; and thy seed shall possess the gate of his enemies; and in thy seed shall all the nations of the earth be blessed; because thou hast obeyed My voice."[3]

3. But now hath He obtained a more excellent ministry, by how much also He is the mediator of a better covenant, which was established upon better promises. For if that first covenant had been faultless, then should no place have been sought for the second. For finding fault with them, He saith, "Behold, the days come," saith the Lord, "when I will make a new covenant with the house of Israel and with the house of Judah: not according to the covenant that I made with their fathers in the day when I took them by the hand to lead them out of the land of Egypt; because they continued not in My covenant, and I regarded them not," saith the Lord. "For this is the covenant that I will make with the house of Israel after those days," saith the Lord, "I will put My laws into their mind, and write them in their hearts: and I will be to them a God, and they shall be to Me a people". In that He saith, a new covenant, He hath made the

first old. Now that which decayeth and waxeth old is ready to vanish away.[4]

Jesus, Our Mediator:

How much more shall the blood of Christ, who through the eternal Spirit offered Himself without spot to God, purge your conscience from dead works to serve the living God? And for this cause He is the mediator of the new testament, that by means of death, for the redemption of the transgressions that were under the first testament, they which are called might receive the promise of eternal inheritance:[5] and to Jesus the mediator of the new covenant, and to the blood of sprinkling, that speaketh better things than that of Abel.[6]

The Abrahamic Covenant Fulfilled:

That the blessing of Abraham might come on the Gentiles through Jesus Christ; that we might receive the promise of the Spirit through faith. Brethren, I speak after the manner of men; though it be but a man's covenant, yet if it be confirmed, no man disannulleth, or addeth thereto. Now to Abraham and his seed were the promises made. He saith not, 'and to seeds,' as of many; but as of one, 'and to thy seed,' which is Christ. And this I say, that the covenant, that was confirmed before of God in Christ, the law, which was four hundred and thirty years after, cannot disannul, that it should make the promise of none effect. For if the inheritance be of the law, it is no more of promise: but God gave it to Abraham by promise. Wherefore serveth the law? It was added because of transgressions, till the seed should come to whom the promise was made; and it was ordained by angels in the hand of a mediator.[7] Now a mediator is not a mediator of one, but God is one. Is the law then against the promises of God? God forbid: for if there had been a law given which could have given life, verily righteousness should have been by the law. But the scripture hath concluded all under sin, that the promise by faith of Jesus Christ might be given to them that believe. But before faith came, we were kept under the law, shut up unto the faith which should afterwards be revealed. Wherefore the law was our schoolmaster to bring us unto Christ, that we might be justified by faith. But after that faith is come, we are no longer under a schoolmaster. For ye are all the children of God by faith in Christ Jesus. For as many of you as have been baptized into Christ have put on Christ. There is neither Jew nor Greek, there is neither bond nor free, there is neither male nor female: for ye are all one in Christ Jesus. And if ye be Christ's, then are ye Abraham's seed, and heirs according to the promise.[8]

For when God made promise to Abraham, because He could swear by no greater, He sware by Himself, saying, "Surely blessing I will bless thee, and multiplying I will multiply thee." And so, after he had patiently endured, he obtained the promise. For men verily swear by the greater: and an oath for confirmation is to them an end of all strife. Wherein God, willing more abundantly to show unto the heirs of promise the immutability of His counsel, confirmed it by an oath: that by two immutable things, in which it was impossible for God to lie, we might have a strong consolation, who have fled for refuge to lay hold upon the hope set before us: which hope we have as an anchor of the soul, both sure and stedfast, and which entereth into that within the veil.[9]

Wherefore, you are no more a servant, but a son; and if a son, then an heir of God through Christ.[10]

References:

1) Ephesians 2:11-13 2) Genesis 9:13,15-16
3) Genesis 22:16-18 4) Hebrews 8:6-10,13 5) Hebrews 9:14,15
6) Hebrews 12:24 7) Galatians 3:14-19
8) Galatians 3:20-29 9) Hebrews 6:13-19
10) Galatians 4:7

CHAPTER 97

YOUR INHERITANCE

Give thanks to the Father, which has made us to be partakers of the inheritance of the saints in light,[1] and if you be Christ's then are you Abraham's seed and heirs according to the promise.[2] Now I say, that the heir, as long as he is a child, differs nothing from a servant, though he be lord of all; but is under tutors and governors until the time appointed of the father. Even so we, when we were children, were in bondage under the elements of the world: but when the fullness of the time was come, God sent forth His Son, made of a woman, made under the law, to redeem them that were under the law, that we might receive the adoption of sons. And because you are sons, God hath sent forth the Spirit of His Son into your hearts, crying, Abba Father.[3]

In whom also we have obtained an inheritance, being predestined according to the purpose of Him who works all things after the counsel of His own will, that we should be to the praise of His glory, who first trusted in Christ. In Whom you also trusted after you heard the word of truth, the gospel of your salvation: in Whom also, after you believed, you were sealed with the Holy Spirit of promise, which is the downpayment of our inheritance until the redemption of the purchased possession, unto the praise of His glory.[4] Have the eyes of your understanding enlightened, that you may know what is the hope of His calling and what is the riches of the glory of His inheritance in the saints.[5]

Know that the unrighteous shall not inherit the kingdom of God. Be not deceived; neither fornicators, nor idolaters, nor adulterers, nor effeminate, nor abusers of themselves with mankind, nor thieves, nor covetous, nor drunkards, nor revilers, nor extortioners, shall inherit the kingdom of God,[6] and no whoremonger, nor unclean person, nor covetous man, who is an idolater, has any inheritance in the kingdom of Christ and of God.[7] Now this I say, brethren, that flesh and blood cannot inherit the kingdom of God; neither doth corruption inherit incorruption.[8]

Blessed be the God and Father of our Lord Jesus Christ, which according to His abundant mercy has begotten us again unto a lively hope by the resurrection of Jesus Christ from the dead, to an inheritance incorruptible, and undefiled, and that fades not away, reserved in heaven for you;[9] knowing that of the Lord you shall receive the reward of the inheritance: for you serve the Lord Christ.[10]

For God has chosen the poor of this world, rich in faith to be heirs of the kingdom which He has promised to them that love Him;[11] and that being justified by His grace, we should be made heirs according to the hope of eternal life.[12]

You are called that you should inherit a blessing[13] as children of God, and if children, then heirs; heirs of God, and joint heirs with Christ, but if we are to share His glory, we must also share His suffering.[14]

God has given angels as ministering spirits sent forth to minister for the heirs of salvation,[15] so be not slothful, but followers of them who through faith and patience inherit the promises.[16] Remember, he that overcomes shall inherit all things, and He will be your God, and you shall be His son.[17]

References:

1) *Colossians 1:12* 2) *Galatians 3:29* 3) *Galatians 4:1-7*
4) *Ephesians 1:11-14* 5) *Ephesians 1:18*
6) *I Corinthians 6:9,10* 7) *Ephesians 5:5*
8) *I Corinthians 15:50* 9) *I Peter 1:3,4* 10) *Colossians 3:24*
11) *James 2:5* 12) *Titus 3:7* 13) *I Peter 3:9*
14) *Romans 8:17* 15) *Hebrews 1:14* 16) *Hebrews 6:12*
17) *Revelation 21:7*

CHAPTER 98

GOD'S FAVOR

Let mercy and truth never leave you; bind them around your neck; write them on the table of your heart. Then you will find favor and good understanding in the sight of God and man.[1] For the Lord will bless the righteous; and surround him like a shield with favor.[2] In His favor is life,[3] making you steady as a mountain.[4]

Blessed is the nation whose God is the Lord; and the people whom He has chosen for His own inheritance.[5] O, taste and see that the Lord is good, and blessed is the man that trusts in Him.[6] In fact, blessed is the man, whose transgression is forgiven,[7] whose sin is not counted against him,[8] who considers the poor,[9] who keeps God's testimonies,[10] and reverences the Lord, walking in His ways,[11] drawing his strength from the Lord,[12] not respecting the proud, nor such as turn aside to lies.[13]

Whoever finds wisdom, finds life, and shall obtain favor of the Lord.[14] And he that diligently seeks good, finds favor,[15] for a good man obtains favor of the Lord.[16] Loving favor is rather to be chosen than silver and gold,[17] and good understanding gives favor.[18] Among the righteous, there is favor,[19] and whoever finds a wife, finds a good thing and obtains favor of the Lord.[20]

The blessing belonging to Abraham came upon the Gentiles through Jesus Christ; that we might receive the promise of the Spirit through faith.[21] So blessed be the God and Father of our Lord Jesus Christ, who has blessed us with all spiritual blessings in heavenly places in Christ.[22] For the blessing of the Lord makes rich, and He adds no sorrow with it.[23] He that has clean hands, and a pure heart; who has not lifted up his soul to vanity, nor sworn deceitfully, he shall receive the blessing from the Lord, and righteousness from the God of his salvation.[24]

How precious are God's thoughts towards you, how great is the sum of hem![25] Whoever touches you, touches the apple of His eye,[26] for great is His mercy toward you.[27] In fact, as the heaven is high above the earth, so great is His mercy toward them that fear Him.[28] For the eye of the Lord is upon them that fear Him, upon them that hope in His mercy.[29]

References:

1) Proverbs 3:3,4   2) Psalms 5:12   3) Psalms 30:5
4) Psalms 30:7   5) Psalms 33:12   6) Psalms 34:8
7) Psalms 32:1   8) Psalms 32:2   9) Psalms 41:1
10) Psalms 119:2   11) Psalms 128:1   12) Psalms 84:5
13) Psalms 40:4   14) Proverbs 8:35   15) Proverbs 11:27
16) Proverbs 12:2   17) Proverbs 22:1   18) Proverbs 13:15
19) Proverbs 14:9   20) Proverbs 18:22
21) Galatians 3:14   22) Ephesians 1:3
23) Proverbs 10:22   24) Psalms 24:4,5   25) Psalms 139:17
26) Zechariah 2:8   27) Psalms 86:13   28) Psalms 103:11
29) Psalms 33:18

CHAPTER 99

THE GOODNESS OF GOD

How great is the goodness, which God has laid up for them that fear Him.[1] The earth is full of the goodness of the Lord,[2] and it endures continually.[3] Oh that men would praise the Lord for His goodness, and for His wonderful works to the children of men! For He satisfies the longing soul, and fills the hungry soul with goodness.[4]

How excellent is His lovingkindness[5] with which He crowns us along with tender mercies.[6] Praise Him, because His lovingkindness is better than life.[7] With this He draws us, for He loves us with an everlasting love.[8] He will restore your soul,[9] your health[10] and all the years that the locust has eaten[11] and heal you of your wounds.[10]

The Lord your God is gracious and merciful, ready to pardon, slow to anger, and of great kindness.[11] He will not forsake you, neither destroy you,[12] nor turn His face from you, if you return to Him,[13] for He is plenteous in mercy,[14] full of compassion,[15] longsuffering, and abundant in goodness and truth.[16] Rend your heart, not your garments, and turn to the Lord your God,[17] and He will be merciful to your unrighteousness, and your sins and iniquities, He will remember no more,[18] for His merciful kindness is great toward us.[19]

The Lord is not slack concerning His promise, as some men count slackness; but is longsuffering toward us, not willing that any should perish, but that all should come to repentance.[20] In fact, there has not failed one word of all His good promise, which He promised by the hand of Moses, His good servant.[21] But God is rich in mercy, for His great love wherewith He loved us,[22] and He will bless them that fear the Lord, both small and great,[23] making rich and adding no sorrow with it.[24] The Lord is mindful of you,[25] and He will bless the righteous and surrounds them with favor like a shield.[26] For the Lord God is a sun and shield providing grace and glory, and no good thing will He withhold from them that walk uprightly.[27] Yes, blessings are upon the head of the just,[28] and among the righteous there is favor[29] and their desire shall be granted.[30]

Many are the afflictions of the righteous, but the Lord delivers him out of them all,[31] for he that trusts in the Lord shall be surrounded with mercy.[32] For the Lord is good, His mercy is everlasting; and His truth endures to all generations.³³ In fact, as the heaven is high above the earth, so great is His mercy toward them that fear Him.³⁴ For I am persuaded that neither death, nor life, nor angels, nor principalities, nor powers, nor things present, nor things to come, nor height, nor depth, nor any other creature, shall be able to separate us from the love of God, which is in Christ Jesus our Lord.³⁵ For the Lord will not cast off His people, neither will He forsake His inheritance,³⁶ neither is there any condemnation to them which are in Christ Jesus, who walk not after the flesh, but after the spirit.³⁷

The Lord will never leave you, nor forsake you.³⁸ He is with you always, even to the end of the world.³⁹ Can a woman forget her sucking child, that she should not have compassion on the son of her womb? Yes, she may forget, but the Lord will not forget you.⁴⁰ In fact, He has graven you upon the palms of His hands,⁴¹ and will perfect that which concerns you.⁴² When you fall, He will raise you up,⁴³ for the Lord upholds the good man with His hand.⁴⁴ When you fall, you will arise,⁴⁵ because greater is He that is in you, than he that is in the world,⁴⁶ which enables you to do all things through Christ who strengthens you.⁴⁷ And surely goodness and mercy shall follow you all the days of your life.⁴⁸

References:

1) *Psalms 31:19 2) Psalms 33:5 3) Psalms 52:1*
4) *Psalms 107:8–9 5) Psalms 36:7 6) Psalms 103:4*
7) *Psalms 63:3 8) Jeremiah 31:3 9) Psalms 23:3*
10) *Jeremiah 30:17 11) Nehemiah 9:17*
12) *Deuteronomy 4:31 13) II Chronicles 30:9*
14) *Psalms 103:8 15) Psalms 111:4 16) Exodus 34:6*
17) *Joel 2:13 18) Hebrews 8:12 19) Psalms 117:2*
20) *II Peter 3:9 21) I Kings 8:56 22) Ephesians 2:4*
23) *Psalms 115:13 24) Proverbs 10:22 25) Psalms 115:12*
26) *Psalms 5:12 27) Psalms 84:11 28) Proverbs 10:6*
29) *Proverbs 14:9 30) Proverbs 10:24 31) Psalms 34:19*
32) *Psalms 32:10 33) Psalms 100:5 34) Psalms 103:11*
35) *Romans 8:38–39 36) Psalms 94:14 37) Romans 8:1*
38) *Hebrews 13:5 39) Matthew 28:20 40) Isaiah 49:15*
41) *Isaiah 49:16 42) Psalms 138:8 43) Psalms 145:14*
44) *Psalms 37:23–24 45) Micah 7:8 46) I John 4:4*
47) *Philippians 4:13 48) Psalms 23:6*

297

CHAPTER 100

HOPE FOR THE FALLEN

Rejoice not against me, O my enemy: when I fall, I shall arise: when I sit in darkness, the Lord shall be a light unto me.[1] For you see, the steps of a good man are ordered by the Lord; and He delights in his way. Though he fall, he shall not be utterly cast down, for the Lord upholds him with His hand.[2] In fact, the Lord upholds all that fall, and raises up all that be bowed down.[3] Yes, a just man falls seven times, and rises up again,[4] and though he walk in the midst of trouble, God will revive him.[5]

For if you turn again unto the Lord, you shall find compassion with your captors and return to your land: for the Lord your God is gracious and merciful, and will not turn away His face from you, if you return to Him.[6] Yes, rend your heart, and not your garments, and turn to the Lord your God: for He is gracious and merciful, slow to anger and of great kindness, and anxious not to punish you.[7] And God will be merciful to your unrighteousness, and your sins and your iniquities will He remember no more.[8] Oh how great is His goodness, which

God has laid up for them that fear Him.⁹ For He satisfies the longing soul and fills the hungry soul with goodness.¹⁰

How excellent is your lovingkindness, O God! Therefore the children of men put their trust under the shadow of your wings.¹¹ Because your lovingkindness is better than life, my lips shall praise You,¹² who redeems my life from destruction; who crowns me with lovingkindness and tender mercies.¹³ For the Lord is not slack concerning His promise, as some men count slackness; but is longsuffering to us, not willing that any should perish, but that all should come to repentance.¹⁴ But God, who is rich in mercy, for His great love wherewith He loved us, even when we were dead in sins, has quickened us together with Christ.¹⁵

Many are the afflictions of the righteous; but the Lord delivers him out of them all.¹⁶ For as the heaven is high above the earth, so great is His mercy toward them that fear Him.¹⁷ And we know, that if we confess our sins, He is faithful and just to forgive us our sins and to cleanse us from all unrighteousness.¹⁸ And He will restore to you the years that the locust has eaten, the cankerworm, and the caterpillar, and the palmerworm.¹⁹

God loved the world so much, that He gave

His only Son, that whoever would believe in Him should not perish but have life everlasting. For God didn't send His Son into the world to condemn it; but that the world through Him might be saved. He that believes on Him is not condemned; but he that doesn't believe is condemned already because he has not believed in the name of the only Son of God.[20]

There is therefore now no condemnation to them which are in Christ Jesus, who walk not after the flesh, but after the Spirit.[21] For the Lord will not cast off His people, neither will he forsake His inheritance,[22] for He has said, "I will never leave you, nor forsake you;[23] lo, I am with you always, even unto the end of the world."[24] Can a woman forget her sucking child, that she should not have compassion on the son of her womb? Yes, she may forget, yet will the Lord not forget you,[25] for He has graven you upon the palms of His hands.[26]

The thief comes only to kill, to steal and to destroy, but Jesus came that we might have life, and that we might have it more abundantly.[27] He didn't come to call the righteous, but the sinners to repentance, for they that are whole have no need of the physician, only those who are sick.[28] He loves us with an everlasting love; drawing us with lovingkindness[29] and will restore unto us the joy of our salvation.[30]

If a man be overtaken in a fault, you which are spiritual, restore such a one in the spirit of meekness; considering yourself, lest you also be tempted.[31] For the Lord restores my soul,[32] and He will perfect that which concerns me; His mercy endures forever.[33] And I am persuaded that neither death nor life, nor angels, nor principalities, nor powers, nor things present, nor things to come, nor height, nor depth, nor any other creature, shall be able to separate me from the love of God, which is in Christ Jesus our Lord.[34]

Remember, you can do all things through Christ who strengthens you,[35] because greater is He that is in you, than he that is in the world.[36]

References:

1) Micah 7:8 2) Psalms 37:23,24 3) Psalms 145:14
4) Proverbs 24:16 5) Psalms 138:7 6) II Chronicles 30:9
7) Joel 2:13 8) Hebrews 8:12 9) Psalms 31:19
10) Psalms 107:9 11) Psalms 36:7 12) Psalms 63:3
13) Psalms 103:4 14) II Peter 3:9 15) Ephesians 2:4,5
16) Psalms 34:19 17) Psalms 103:11 18) I John 1:9
19) Joel 2:25 20) John 3:16-18 21) Romans 8:1
22) Psalms 94:14 23) Hebrews 13:5 24) Matthew 28:20
25) Isaiah 49:15 26) Isaiah 49:16 27) John 10:10
28) Mark 2:17 29) Jeremiah 31:3 30) Psalms 51:12
31) Galatians 6:1 32) Psalms 23:3 33) Psalms 138:8
34) Romans 8:38,39 35) Philippians 4:13 36) I John 4:4

CHAPTER 101

HEALING FOR THE BROKENHEARTED

God heals the broken in heart, and binds up their wounds.[1] Though your father and mother forsake you, the Lord will welcome and comfort you.[2] Can a woman forget her sucking child, that she should not have compassion on the son of her womb? Yes, she may forget, yet will I not forget you.[3] Behold, I have graven you on the palms of My hands; thy walls are continually before Me.[4] For the Lord thy God is a merciful God; He will not forsake you, neither destroy you, nor forget the covenant of your fathers which He sware unto them.[5] For the Lord will not cast off His people, neither will He forsake His inheritance.[6]

The Spirit of the Lord was upon Jesus. He was anointed to preach the gospel to the poor, to heal the brokenhearted, to preach deliverance to the captives, and recovering of sight to the blind, to set at liberty them that are bruised,[7] and He was wounded for our transgressions, bruised for our iniquities: the chastisement of our peace was upon Him; and with His stripes we are healed.[8]

Why is your soul cast down? Why are you disquieted? Hope in God! And praise Him who is the health of your countenance, and your God.[9] You will return and come with singing unto Zion; and everlasting joy shall be upon your head: you shall obtain gladness and joy; and sorrow and mourning shall flee away.[10]

The steps of a good man are ordered by the Lord, and He delights in his way. Though he falls, he shall not be utterly cast down: for the Lord upholds him with His hand.[11] Rejoice not against me, O mine enemy. When I fall, I shall arise; when I sit in darkness, the Lord shall be a light unto me.[12]

When you pass through the waters, God will be with you; and through the rivers, they shall not overflow you; when you walk through the fire, you shall not be burned; neither shall the flame kindle upon you.[13] Fear not, for God is with you: be not dismayed for He is your God: He will strengthen you; yes, He will help you; yes, He will uphold you with the right hand of His righteousness.[14]

They that know Thy name will put their

trust in Thee: for Thou, Lord, have not forsaken them that seek Thee.[15] In fact, you will never leave us, nor forsake us;[16] lo, You are with us always, even unto the end.[17] We may be persecuted, but not forsaken; cast down, but not destroyed.[18] For I am persuaded, that neither death, nor life, nor angels, nor principalities, nor powers, nor things present, nor things to come, nor height, nor depth, nor any other creature, shall be able to separate us from the love of God, which is in Christ Jesus our Lord.[19]

Blessed be God, even the Father of our Lord Jesus Christ, the Father of mercies, and the God of all comfort; who comforts us in all our tribulation, that we may be able to comfort them which are in any trouble, by the comfort wherewith we ourselves are comforted of God.[20] And this is my comfort in affliction, promises from God's word that give me life.[21]

References:

1) Psalms 147:3   2) Psalms 27:10   3) Isaiah 49:15
4) Isaiah 49:16   5) Deuteronomy 4:31   6) Psalms 94:14
7) Luke 4:18   8) Isaiah 53:5   9) Psalms 43:5
10) Isaiah 51:11   11) Psalms 37:23,24   12) Micah 7:8
13) Isaiah 43:2   14) Isaiah 41:10   15) Psalms 9:10
16) Hebrews 13:5   17) Matthew 28:20
18) II Corinthians 4:9   19) Romans 8:38
20) II Corinthians 1:3,4   21) Psalms 119:50

FINAL NOTE

Whereas man usually looks upon the outside, God always looks upon your heart. If you have sincerely turned your life over to Jesus, believing that God raised Him from the dead, and you're not ashamed of Him but confess Him openly, then and only then, do you have eternal salvation. No crime committed, no matter how heinous, no sin or immoral act that you may have done is beyond God's forgiveness, and in accepting that forgiveness, nothing can keep you from eternal life with the Father.

On the other hand, if you deny that Jesus is the Son of God, and you are ashamed to confess Him before others as your Savior, then no righteous act or noble lifestyle, church attendance, baptism, christening, or even generous acts of giving, will gain you entrance into eternal life with the Father, God.

If you're not sure where you stand, or where you would spend eternity if you died tonight, then I urge you, in your own words, in your own way, straight from your heart, ask God to forgive all of your sins and become Lord of your life.